What Matters
MOST

What Matters MOST

EMBRACING
LIFE'S CONNECTIONS
& COMPLICATIONS

LINDA F. HULING

Printed in the United States of America.

ISBN: 978-1-63385-490-1
Library of Congress Control Number: 2023906652

Published by
Word Association Publishers
205 Fifth Avenue
Tarentum, Pennsylvania 15084

www.wordassociation.com
1.800.827.7903

Dedication

For Kathryn and Jared,
Because you have always been my "heart's desire".

Contents

Introduction

"To see a world in a grain of sand, and heaven in a wild flower." William Blake

"All that I hope to say in books, all that I ever hope to say, is that I love the world." E. B. White

Poetry and prose captured my heart when I was very young. Phrases written just so and books I never wanted to end ignited my own desire to write.

Decades of life shaped the words in this book, the stories behind them, and the one who wrote it.

What Matters Most is a letter of love and faith, grounded in all types of relationships...and our connection to each other, ideas, animals, nature, God.

It is a book of reflections, perspectives, devotions, poetry, and prayers. It is a collection of the things we contemplate, analyze, and even laugh about when life's critical moments come to call.

I have always wanted to write the words that caused someone to think, feel, connect. I hope all those things happen for you when you read *What Matters Most.*

Most of all, I hope this book causes you to laugh out loud, to pause and ponder something dear to your heart, to connect with family and friends, to see life differently, or move you to be what you wanted to be all along.

In our endless search for connection, may we find and hold on to what matters most.

The writing of this book was fueled by fresh air, caffeine, and lemon water. It was powered by prayer, inspired by early morning sunrises, evening sunsets, late-night sky-gazing, and a whole lot of daydreaming.

Acknowledgments

Writing is exhilarating, fulfilling, and humbling. I have been all over the place with emotions, ideas, questions as I wrote *What Matters Most.* Along the way, words of support offered to me were better than caffeine and surpassed the highs of chocolate.

So, anyone listed in this acknowledgment section is there for big reasons, not all of which are listed. Just know you made a difference to me.

I am fortunate to be surrounded by an abundance of love from family, friends, and friends who have become family. Thank you is not enough, but I'm going to try.

My children and their spouses, Jared and Lu, Kathryn and Josh: you are the greatest joys in my life. You are the motivation behind this book. Jared and Lu, your support keeps me going. Thank you, Kathryn. I completely trust your discerning comments and am grateful for the micro-Word manual you wrote just for me. I'm thankful to her husband,

Josh, who was instrumental in bringing my blog, Around the Table, to life a couple of years ago, and the one who answers 90% of my technology questions.

I am grateful to the world's best sisters, Jerry and Lettie! You listen, encourage, offer insightful opinions, and care deeply. You have been the cheerleaders in my life. I love and admire you!

What else would I need? Well, cousins who read your stuff are a bonus. I have a soul-sister relationship with my cousin Betsy. From the first time her sassy 8-year-old self joined me on one of my high school dates, we have been singing "It takes Two, Baby" all through life. Thank you also to cousins Toni and Lane, regular readers of Around the Table. I love to hear what you have to say on any topic and appreciate your kind words.

There are so many rotten jokes about in-laws, but I can say that I have the perfect picks in all categories! Jim and Ed (husbands to my sisters), you have been such real brothers to me. Jim, I look forward to our early morning talks in your kitchen. Ed, your love and zany humor have bolstered me for decades. Ann, Hal, Peter, Karen--your prayers and loving care have been there for me since 1984. These 6 human beings mean the world to me.

My parents Chester and Geraldine Floyd were beautiful role models of unconditional love and faith. I stand on solid ground because of them.

Cathy-From walking through old cemeteries 25 years ago, gathering names for my "some-day" novel, providing comments on difficult passages, to making house calls on computer problems, you have been here for the long haul on this book. Thank you, my friend.

Cathy, Colleen, Loreta, Judy-We have spent many evenings by the fire pit, on patios, decks, and around kitchen tables. We dance together, play games till the wee hours, share confidences and heartaches. We cheer each other on and applaud each other's children. Thank you for all of that and for the confidence you have given me to get this done.

Lori, Jeanne, Helen, Mary, Nancy, Linda W, Sandy-Our circle came together a couple of decades ago. We have discussed every topic under the sun, solved a million problems, counseled, and encouraged each other, shared wine and dreams. My life is richer for having known each of you.

Pat G, Terrie Q, Elaine, David, Mel, Brenda Jo, Mari, Debbie, Mary Beth C., Gretchen - Your words encourage me; your prayers and complete support mean the world to me.

Pastor Bud, thank you for having faith in me and giving me the opportunity to write devotions for our church in 2019. That was a launch all its own and an important step for me.

Jason, I admire your expertise in design and technology. Thank you for your creativity, kindness, patience and problem-solving skills. I would still be "googling" how to get that first manuscript sent if not for you.

April, thank you for your work on the design elements of this book. I appreciate your willingness to jump right in with such energy and professionalism.

Francine, owner of Word Association Publishers, thank you for writing the back cover text. I appreciate having your expert skill on this and feel like I have connected with another kindred soul.

Tom, owner of Word Association Publishers and my editor, thank you for all the enlightening conversations and excellent guidance, for challenging me, and of course your editing wisdom. Every time I receive your notes, I thank my lucky stars that you are my editor.

And grateful thanks to God, the Father, Son, and Holy Spirit, who always shows up and tenderly leads me to what matters most.

Part One:

What We Learn from Wonder

Place Holder Dreams

As soon as I got my license and my rare opportunity with the family car, I hightailed it to Lowndes Hill, the hill that overlooked my hometown. Notebook in hand, two finely sharpened pencils and a Bic along for the ride, I sat on my favorite tree stump near the moss, packed my emotions into some teenage poetry, and scribbled my dreams in the margins.

Big dreams about love, writing, creating, acting, singing, teaching and travel beyond my West Virginia hills filled my notebooks and my nights.

Decades later, having accomplished an entirely different life than I ever dreamed about, I still longed for a few of those by-passed plans. They call my name when I let my mind drift and dream.

I think we all have those persistent dreams tucked away in the folds of our memories.

Close your eyes and imagine your future. What do you see?

Is there something that keeps calling **your** name every time you let your mind drift?

Life dreams, the big ones!

Do you keep pushing your dream off to the side in a kind of place holder position?

I'm talking about the place where dreams go to sleep.

I call these **Place Holder Dreams!**

We **ALL** have those hopes that we just can't get out of the notebook and off the ground!

Wonderful, incredibly exciting nuggets for the next stage in our lives, still floundering in the planning stages.

These dreams hold a place in our hearts and minds while they tug at our most creative parts, straining to be heard, and fighting to be put in first place.

And yet we keep them silent and still.

How is it that we lose sight of our prized dreams so easily?

How do those dreams get shifted down into low priority lanes?

Place Holder Dreams are too important to let them get discarded in the waste bin of our mind's eye.

And yet sometimes that's exactly where they end up.

I know this because I put too many of my own dreams in that holding bin for too long.

I have kept some of mine alive for decades, just barely breathing.

One of them finally made it into the real world right after Thanksgiving, 2019.

And part two of this same dream was launched on Valentine's Day, 2020.

It was the dream of putting my writing "out there in the world" beyond the safety of friends and family.

Here's what happened when I jumped in to save my Dream from waste bin suffocation.

To be upfront about this, "jumped in" is not exactly accurate. It was more "tippy-toeing" in after I was given a little boost in the seat of the pants. Ok, I admit it. It was a kick in the pants, albeit a metaphorical one.

While I was holding the dream of publishing in that Place Holder Position, I kept writing pieces here and there, randomly posting on Facebook.

Occasionally, some of the pieces were about faith.

My pastor, Bud Leskovac, read some of those and asked me to write a series of Advent Devotions based on the book of Luke for the 2019 Christmas season.

His words were "I'd like you to consider doing this for the church. And I know you can do it." How could I say no to that?

Immediately, I was excited by his request, motivated by something much bigger than myself.

That's what started the unearthing of my place holder dream…someone who believed in me enough to offer an opportunity.

He set a deadline, a few guidelines, gave me a one-minute pep talk and set me to it.

And just like that, I was on the road to a big writing project.

YOU DON'T NEED WARRIOR SHOES! JUST A LITTLE FAITH!

Full disclosure here, my initial **launch** is **NOT** a story of bravery.

Courage came after the "launch" …the moment I picked up my pen …and then quickly switched to my computer. It's easier to type on a keyboard when your nerves are on edge than it is to hold a pen.

Very soon I settled down and settled into some of the most joyous hours of my creative life. It was thrilling.

I believe that's how you know you're moving through the force of a well-matched life dream.

You are immersed, committed. You are stretching every part of your skills, talents and courage. And you are living in pure joy. Even frequent angst doesn't hold you back.

Yes, there is angst. Yes, there is the constant editing and the ever-present fear of rejection. Those parts really don't go away, at least not for me yet.

But these things are taking the back seat now, not the dream.

When your dream finally comes forward and owns its place in your timeline, you feel the thrill of bringing something to life. And that victory is sweet!

Psychologists are right. Actualization brings amazing satisfaction!

And with that, comes the courage to step out again.

I launched my blog, **Around the Table**, on February 14, 2020 because my enthusiastic son-in-law, Josh, said to me that day, "Let's get this thing online!" I had written the introduction weeks before, chosen a few photos but was stalling in place. So, he flashed his brilliant smile and he proceeded to techno-wizard me through the WordPress launch.

Thank heaven for Millennials and their fearless technical skills. Gotta love 'em!

I wear Baby Boomer shoes but I'm still operating in baby steps. Sometimes I need to be challenged. Both Bud and Josh challenged me in their own unique ways. I am grateful.

Speaking of baby steps and challenges, I think the way babies learn to crawl is the perfect simile of how we take our Place Holder Dreams out of inertia and ease them on their way to the launchpad.

Picture the steps of how a baby learns to crawl.

(1) First, there is always a reason for that baby to **WANT** to move forward.

The motivation is sometimes a favorite toy or treat, but more often it is the smiling face of a parent or grandparent, encouraging them all the way.

I'm calling this the squad of encouragers… the Cheerleaders in our lives.

(2) Eventually, babies get enough strength to pull their front bodies up off of the ground and support themselves on their own.

It is a gathering of steam and strength, a blend of courage and confidence.

(3) Next, they start the rhythmic movement of rocking their bodies a little forward and a little backward. They realize they need to leave the safety of that one place because they want what is ahead of them.

They respond to the pull of desire and reward.

(4) Eventually they lift one knee off of the ground and edge forward, followed by the other knee, smiling

all the way, as they rock & roll their way to their destination.

Success! A little success creates more success. And on they go.

A baby overcomes inertia because she stops **holding** herself in **one place** and puts her **dream** out in front of her!

This may have been the 101st time she tried this feat.

Babies are brilliant, but they don't learn to crawl in one day.

Neither do we become successful at launching our dreams overnight.

But when we finally take that dream out of hiding and put it out in front of us, a little part of us grows. And there's nothing like growing and stretching in every part of our lives…young, middle, older. There's always room to grow and a place to shine.

Do you have a Place Holder Dream?

Is it time to move it out of storage and into FIRST PLACE?

Sometimes we get off track, for a day, a year, or even a few decades.

Sometimes we can get back on track with just one change of heart.

We might need a reframing of our dream or our attitude, maybe some realism.

We might need to bring forward our most positive self.

Or maybe we finally listen to a trusted and faithful friend, or family member who has never once given up on you or your dream.

That kind of encouragement is priceless.

That kind of support builds solid dreams that won't fail.

LISTEN TO THE CHEERLEADERS!

Listen to those who have traveled this road with you; those who have encouraged you to take just one step forward out of the place holder spot.

They know you and have your best interests at heart.

Give their words airtime in your head!

I am blessed with generous people in my life who will offer constructive feedback for me from time to time. There are three in particular who have been long time, faithful readers of my sentences, whose comments are genuine, thoughtful, and honest. They are my daughter, Kathryn, my friend Cathy, and my sister Lettie. I can always trust what they say. When I'm stuck, I go to them.

You may have people like that too in your life. Ask them. Their comments are worth gold.

If you have not yet found your trusted others, then, by all means, trust yourself.

Trust the instincts that have faithfully guided you all along your pathway.

I hope this post encourages you to take a risk; expect the unexpected; step out into the unknown, get uncomfortable, and move toward hope and a whole lot of faith in yourself!

As my sister-in-law, Ann, reminded me in 2020, "It's Leap Year, you know! Just take a leap!"

Waiting for the perfect time is a waste of time.

Right now, is the perfect time to say "Yes" to your dream! And perhaps for the first time in your life, put your dream in first place.

When We Were Young and Glorious

Too little is said these days of the thrill of being able to put one foot in front of the other.

I mean, putting one foot in front of the other WITHOUT any pain.

Ah! The good old days when we were young and glorious!

Remember when we did not even think about walking or any movement for that matter.

We just got up and out, and on to the next thing.

Remember when we could work a 12-hour day, run 4 miles, then play tennis till midnight.

And sleep! Remember Sleep! As in all night long, no interruptions!

I remember fast forwarding the DVR past the ads for heartburn, cataracts, and arthritis, smugly thinking,

"That'll NEVER happen!" Then waking up one morning and realizing you actually have 2 out of 3 of those ailments and maybe a few others tacked on as well.

Have you caught yourself riffling through photos from your 20's & 30's, even 40's & 50's thinking...why didn't I know what I had back then? Why didn't I appreciate what I could do, and how I could move?

A wise friend of mine likes to say, "The older I get, the better I used to look." Her name is Brenda Jo. And Brenda Jo is not one to dwell on the negative, not at all. She has lived a wonderful, joyful life despite enduring one of life's cruelest turns.

I love her attitude of looking back and smiling, not regretting. She looks back with laughter and fondness for "young Brenda." But I don't get the feeling that she wishes she were still back there. I get the feeling that she knows her younger self was busy building family and career memories, character, and lifelong friendships to cherish. Older, wiser Brenda now gets to reap the harvest of that glorious, cherished past.

In fact, the word, "cherish" reminds me of 14-year-old Brenda and the sweet, innocent 1966 song, "Cherish" by The Association. It was one of her favorite tunes in junior high.

She has always known just what to cherish, what to keep, and what to let go of.

Today's Brenda holds her head up high, despite knees that cannot quite keep up with her energy. She keeps moving, one foot in front of the other, day after day, finding joy in the present and seeking new adventures. She has planned many trips for this year and beyond and she is still holding some days open for me to visit her down south in Dixie!

I can't wait!

Aches and pains of aging, notwithstanding, here's to keeping good perspectives as we age.

Here's to looking back with fondness and not regret.

Here's to the Brendas of the world and their "touch your heart" smiles.

MORAL OF THE STORY:

If you are this day young and glorious, then take note, take time to enjoy it, and for goodness' sake, take pictures!

This piece is dedicated to the ageless YOUNG AT HEART!

Take a look at the words to one of my favorite songs,

"Young at Heart" (lyrics by Carolyn Leigh and Johnny Richards)

Find this song on YouTube and listen to it soon.

It will put you in the best mood! I promise!

These are the lines that are forever stuck in my head.

"And if you should survive to a hundred and five
Look at all you'll derive out of being alive.
And here is the best part, you have a head start,
If you are among the very young at heart."

Sweet Flower Revival!

I finally gave up. Tired of watering a brown and bloomless plant, I had to face the fact that my show-stopping dianthus was not just very, very dry. It was dead.

Deciding to move it temporarily to a mini-compost bucket off of my deck, I figured the least I could do would be to give this plant a break from the sun, if not its rightful burial.

Moving too fast for the flip-flops I sported, I tripped and dropped the whole thing. My favorite pot shattered into tiny clay pieces, making a big mess even worse. The dianthus was barely hanging on by its roots and a few clumps of dry dirt.

I tossed what was left of the plant on top of the make-shift compost bucket outside my deck and cleaned up the mess of a million cobalt blue shards. I needed to address the mess on my deck and move on to the rest of my TO DO list.

One sunset followed another and soon I forgot about the upended dianthus. After weeks of blistering temperatures, the rains finally came and stayed for days on end. I turned this monsoon time to weeding in between downpours. Meanwhile, lost in the process were the remains of a dying dianthus on the side of a deck.

The day the sun returned I was cleaning the mildew and algae on my deck when a profusion of pink caught my eye on the other side of the railing. Tiny blooms were triumphant where once I had discarded the mess. My dianthus had risen from the dead!

So, I replanted it into another blue pot, using all the soil it seemed to like, pruned the dead parts, and placed the miraculous dianthus back on the deck to try once more.

The second time around had produced a brighter, healthier dianthus than before.

It's now mid-September and I'm still enjoying this sweet flower revival story.

Second chances...we all deserve them.

But we don't always get the opportunity to try again in a different place, in richer soil.

We aren't always wise enough to know when we need the sun and when we need the rain.

When all around you, the broken pieces look like far too many to fix, perhaps the message is to start over.

Sometimes we need to stop fixating on "what was" or "what should have been," and start fixing our eyes on "what is."

And I think of the rare but golden times when life hands us something unusually good and we are given another go at life and love.

Today, wherever you and I are in our lives, we need to know that it is never too late. Revival is a wonderful thing.

As long as we have breath, we cannot give up!

The autumn of our lives can be just as rewarding and beautiful as the spring!

Believe in second chances.
Expect the unexpected.
I know I am.

The Beauty of Knowing

"Whether you turn to the right or to the left, your ears will hear a voice behind you, saying, "This is the way; walk in it." Isaiah 30:21

We long to hear the voice of God, to know His direction in our lives.

And so, we pray for that and for ears tuned to hear Him when He calls.

Those times in your life when you know without any doubt that God is urging you toward or away from something are amazing and rare.

What about the times when the callings are so soft, so subtle that we can miss them, even when they are right in front of our faces?

I'm thinking about the times when a friend "pops" into your mind randomly; or when a Facebook friend's post screams at you to respond; or when taking your grocery cart to the corral seems too much in the cold winter wind, but you know you have to do it.

I don't think these things are just about doing the right thing. I think they are even more than that.

I think it is the way we learn to "hear" God if we choose to. And if true, then this makes them big things. How many of us have said, "If only I could hear God talking to me, I would know what to do. I would know His Will for my life."

I don't think these are random happenings; nor do I think they are small. They are openings to "listen"; divine opportunities to decide what we do or not do.

It is not that we don't see these openings, but that we "miss" them because we let schedules, to-do lists, or our own stubbornness keep us from responding.

I am reminded of the richness of these nudgings from God by the times when we think our purpose that day is one thing, but God has another, or we set out to address one layer of a problem, and God has the entire onion in mind.

God turns our thinking upside down at times.

We may be having coffee with a friend, reaching out to help them through a difficult time and in addition we may find the answer to our own prayers in the words spoken by that friend. God may have nudged us to contact this friend, only to work a dual blessing for both.

It makes sense that if we practice listening and paying attention to the divine nudgings from the Holy Spirit, then we will get better at recognizing His Voice and eventually His Will for us.

What do we miss when we choose to ignore those quiet "callings" from God?

And what do we gain when we heed them?

All around us, "to the right and to the left", there are messages from God, calling us closer to Him, calling us to respond, to speak up, write, to act.

Oh, that we would use our ears to hear, eyes to see, and hands to do that which is right in front of us.

Then we would know the Way, and we would walk in it.

Take Five!

When was the last time you paused in the middle of a huge project and just sat down, or put down your pen, or walked away from the keyboard? When was the last time you took a break, even just a little break from work, from parenting, from adulting--all those HVAC problems, or the dreaded water/mold issues. What would it be like to take a break from the weariness of life and all its pressures and expectations?

Life's full-on high bar of performance seems so out of reach these days.
We are weary, tired, and tired of being weary.
Maybe you are weary of being both mom AND manager, dad and dentist, teacher, plumber, designer.
Maybe you're single and you have to do it ALL by yourself, every single thing!

Maybe you're retired and all those health insurance decisions have given you a permanent headache and the feeling of cherry pits in your gut. Or maybe you just found out those cherry pits are actually kidney stones.

So, what do you when you can't get up from the floor of exhaustion?
What do you do when your momentum has moved on.
When you can't find your keys, much less your center?
When your phone is as frozen as your heart.
You are done!
You have nothing left to give!
You dare anyone to ask for "just this one little thing".

NO!

From somewhere deep inside you comes that monosyllabic word…NO!

And just like that, you have found the beginning of your way up and out.
The word "no".

It is one of life's greatest stress management tools.

You can find a million ways to say it, some tactful, some not so much.
Some brief…some laced with 20 more words.

The bottom line when you are bottomed out is finding your line of demarcation.

Finding your own way to place a boundary between the harried and jumbled mess you were in and the resting place to figure out what steps lie ahead.

Because we live such calendar filled lives, most of us will recognize the need to stop, but choose to jump from one pile of mess to the next one, just as messy, and just as piled up. It's hard to see any other way if that's the only way we have operated for years.

The old definition of insanity comes to mind...doing the same thing over and over, expecting different results, yada, yada. We know that, but we do it anyway. So, we continue to hyper-jump from pile to pile...one mess and one hypertension med to another.

We're too tired to figure out another way. We can't see past the chaos because there are just too many piles in our way.

Until we rediscover the power of "No", the power of the pause.

Are we brave enough to do it? Brave enough to go through with the follow through and all that means?

Taking risks is risky business.

But the alternatives are risky too. When we can't get off the merry-go round, we tend to get sick.

The first time you say "no" to something or someone you have always said "yes" to is the hardest, scariest, most unsettling thing.

It can also be the most relief-filled moment.
It will feel as if you have caught your breath, as you regain your sanity.
It is energy-renewing and satisfying.

What to do in the pause between?
Nothing. Absolutely nothing. Don't be tempted to fill space.

Soak up the calm atmosphere. Let relief and relaxation flow through your body and mind.
Enjoy the quiet.

In this place you will find perspective.
In this place you will find creativity.
In this place you will find the sweet spot of invigoration.

This is where you land for a while, regenerate.
It's where you'll find the motivation to move on to the next thing...from a position of renewed strength and purpose.
This is a good place to be and a good place from which to rejoin with a resounding "YES".

Throw Wide the Windows!

Throw wide the windows!

Slide the glass door open!

Spring has burst through and set the calendar aright.

Listen!

Can you hear the sounds of spring in the marshes, along the hiking trails, in the matted woods, and on the walkway to your porch?

Rowdy frogs and baby birds are singing the story of resilient rebirth and restorative hope.

Catch the familiar signs of spring, coming up and through and out.

Linger along the path and find the mini bluets competing with regal bluebells. The white miner's lettuce with their lavender stripes, reside alongside deep indigo violets and their Irish-gilded leaves, begging to be noticed.

Tucked in and around nature's piney mulch, and under the vining, they're waiting ... waiting to be seen.

Can you smell the fruitiness of grape hyacinths, the musky smell of moss and loam, or the earthy scent of the woods' prized leaf mulch?

Can you feel the heartbeat of lovers, holding hands... the pull of their attraction as they sway to the song of the nightingale? Can you remember your own long ago shared whisper in the woods?

Savor the memories, feel the breeze, and clear the webs of winter.

On days like today when the air is so full and fresh and the rays of sunlight so golden, I am filled with possibilities.

The outlook doesn't seem so dire, the future not so bare.

There is promise all around and in the air.

Ah, Spring! We've been waiting for you!

Dare to Believe

I am reading Mark 5:24-43 this morning in multiple versions, doing what I love to do, looking at all the different choices of words, different "takes" on what happened long ago.

I learn something new each time with each version. One of them in particular was calling my name today. Jesus's words always pierce our understanding as well as our hearts when we come to Him with an open mind.

In one version, His words to a woman who had suffered in health for 12 years were as directive as they were comforting. "Daughter, because you dared to believe, your faith has healed you. Go with peace in your heart, and be free from your suffering."

He tells her how faith has worked in her healing and then tells her how to live the rest of her days. A big message in just a few verses.

We come to Him with our own personal, singular problem and He leaves us with a plan to heal the whole of us. What a savior!

Just a paragraph or two later Jesus is told by a messenger from another man's house that the little daughter of Jairus has died and there is no need for Jesus to come anymore. But Jesus will have none of that! He instructs the messenger with these powerful words that we would be right in heeding today, "Don't yield to fear. All you need to do is keep believing."

And then Jesus proceeds to perform the miracle that opened so many eyes...He brings that little girl back to life with these words, "Little girl, wake up from the sleep of death."

Wake up from the sleep of death!

Oh, yes!! Indeed, let's wake up from the sleep of death that paralyzes and holds us back.

Wake up and walk into a new life, whole again.

Dare to believe and in so doing, heal!

Father, create in us hearts to dare, courage to care, and faith to believe!

Amen.

Decisions! Decisions! Decisions!

What to do about what kept you awake last night?

What to do about the endless "To Do" list.

If only we had expert advice on how to approach something or someone right at our fingertips, life would be so much easier.

If we could just see a bit into the future to know which road to take, which job to say yes to, which caregiver for our precious children was the best one, what retirement plan to embrace, and even what to do after we retire, our decisions would not only be smarter, but so much wiser.

The difficulty of knowing which words to say, or not say to those we love, can tear us apart.

And the hardest part of parenting...our role as parents of adult children...goodness, wasn't that a surprise? I could certainly use a little help in this.

There isn't a time in my life when I didn't desire some divine insight on something I was dealing with at that moment. A little help, a nudge in the right direction, or a sign to keep my mouth discreetly and tightly closed.

At every crossroads, initially I have felt I was on my own with those decisions, all alone and floundering.

But that's not the truth of it. Even if there is no human being walking alongside me, I am never really alone. The best source of wisdom is right at my fingertips.

James, the brother of Jesus, and leader of the Jerusalem council, writes in his letter to the 12 tribes, "If any of you lacks wisdom, he should ask God, who gives generously to all without finding fault, and it will be given to him." (James 1:5)

Look at these words! Not one word is wasted here.

I love that he begins this first sentence with the word "IF".

He knows we need wisdom, but he chooses the word IF.

I think that is because we have to know and admit that we need help, in order to be in the best position to receive it.

Some of us think we have to manage all of our stuff by ourselves. He knows that; loves us anyway and is patient to wait on us to find that we need to ask for some help.

So, once we decide we can't do this ourselves, our next step is to ask someone. We can choose to Google, which is always a "go to" for me. We can dial a friend, another thing I do frequently. And we can also bring God into the mix simply by asking him for wisdom.

Usually, this the LAST thing we do.

Think what would happen if we did this one FIRST!

One of the best benefits of asking God first, is that He is going to give us all we need because He truly is generous and He is never going to shame us for not knowing. He is not going to find fault in our faulty thinking. He's just going to give fully when we ask.

If we are open to all of this, the wisdom will flow, from the pages of His Word, or from answers to our prayers, or both.

Those answers can come in many forms. You may truly hear a whisper in your heart, or words from a friend will strike a chord with you, or you may read something insightful. You may receive a card in the mail with just the right message for you. God works in mysterious ways, but we need to be open to receiving the mystery and acknowledge it is from Him.

Just like that, and so many other ways, divine wisdom will be ours.

A grateful, acknowledging heart keeps the communication flowing.

Thank you, generous and loving Lord, for this eternal pipeline straight to you; and for your gracious gifts, ready for us, any time, night or day. Amen.

In the Shadow of Mercy

Wherever I go, she follows me.

I try to out run, out think, out stay her, but she's too close and too fine a partner to be fooled.

I look outside myself for answers, but she looks within.

She knows me…all the ugly things and the intolerant things…she's seen them, heard them, felt them and yet she stays.

She rides a wave of self-criticism with me, sinks to the lowest depths of despair. And still she's there.

She is by my side as I trail down a path of pain.

I throw my compass into a thickened forest of lies.
She feels the weight of my lost soul.
And yet she remains.

It is a miracle that she does, as I have rejected her ways for many years now.

She is my shield of goodness.
She is the one who listens to the constant tape in my head:
"You're not good enough."
"You can't get out of this mess."
"You are alone."
"Everything is too hard and I'm just so tired."
"Nothing matters. Don't bother getting up."

Destructive words darken my thoughts and slowly destroy my future.

But she is having none of that! None!

She knows words are power!
They are dynamite used either to destroy or to shape our next steps.
And the difference between the two outcomes is tenuous.

She knows there is no magic word to right this wrong, no drug to dim the pain and smooth the edges. But she knows in the end good will somehow win over evil. And this is what I need to hear.

I am not alone in this battle now.

My partner's name is Mercy, wise and determined, she is a gift from God when I need it most. She has never given up on me.

She is a splash of cool water on hot and fevered cheeks.

She knows who the real enemy is and she knows this battle will be as complicated as it will be fierce.

And so, she moves with great agility, arms herself with truth, gentleness, and the clarity of knowledge.

Her words are soft but sure.

"Your life has purpose and meaning.
You don't have to figure it out all at once. You just need to begin."

"You must drive out the lies you are living by, cast away weak excuses and old habits, and open up to truth."

She whispers, "But…First forgive!"

And as I yield to the healing power of forgiveness, layers of lies and doubt are shaken far and wide.
Seeds of confidence and determination take their place.

Facades fall short in the presence of Truth.
Insecurities pale in the shadow of Mercy.

The way of mercy leads to forgiveness and forgiveness leads to freedom.

And finally, the door to hope and desire is thrown open.

I speak these words out loud so I can be surrounded by their strength.

I need to hope and love again.

I want to be who I was meant to be

I speak confidently now to the Present, to the Future…

"For surely goodness and mercy shall follow me all the days of my life." Psalm 23:6

Grounded Strength

I wish I could give you the peace of a cool night sky or early morning air.

I wish I could offer the strength of mountains, the consistency of constellations, and the flexibility of the moon.

I would if I could.

I would grab the power of the moment when good friends connect, becoming great friends over the years, and I would freeze that moment just so you would know it would always be there for you.

I would capture years of joy and laughter, an accumulation of only the finest times to be conjured just when you need them. I would give you the memories of the times when eight women were their best, and rallied around each other, marched together for equal rights, sat by hospital bedsides, talked into the night until problems were solved, and hearts were healed.

I would give all of this to you if I could.

We all would. All your sisters would petition the world for your best life if we could.

Yet, please know this: You have all that you need at your own capable fingertips.

Your strength and courage lie at the ready, in the depth of your being!

Hold on, my friend.

Healing is there and is coming in waves of grounded strength.

Just for you! Because you *can*!

What Lies Beneath

Every time I learn of someone else's very real, very raw life journey, the ones who have been "through it and back", I am stopped in my tracks, in awe of human resilience.

I find myself thinking about their stories and reliving them in my mind, stories of tragedy, the loss of a husband in his prime, the abuse of a child at the hands of someone they trusted, the cancer that took everything, the teenager who never bathes so that her mother's boyfriend leaves her alone, the mother who has lost her child to a gunshot wound in the schoolroom.

These are the people who have every reason not to get up after they've been knocked down, and yet somehow, they do.

The act of resilience after devastating loss is more than inspiring. It is the behavior that changes everything. It is the behavior that marks strength and courage beyond understanding.

Pain and resilience shouldered in silence create silent heroes, that may appear to the world like they have moved on with their lives. And that's anything but true.

Drive a little closer to the edge of their lives and you come away with a piece of their hard reality, the loss that they hide from others. Once they let you in and share their stories, you may find detailed images so graphic and moving that it takes a while to reach even keel after hearing it all.

It's like the gut-wrenching feeling of tilting over too far on two wheels and straining to right the balance. You never quite catch your breath after that.

But some stories are never told, because they are covered over with an invisible shield and a pretend smile.

You can't see through the shield and you're not even sure it exists.

As a matter of fact, you may have missed it entirely. But it's there.

And the story waits to be told till someone can see beyond the smile to what lies within.

When you are allowed to see the view behind the smile, you uncover complexity, complications, and raw cross sections of pain.

And when you listen with your heart to their words, see with empathy and understanding, then you get the *real* story, the one that lies beneath.

It takes effort and commitment to see beyond the shield.

You come to understand what has made that person who he is, who she is.

You come to understand all the work that has gone into their ongoing recovery from tragedy.

And if you have won their trust, the shield eventually fades in your presence. Trust needs to be carefully held. One small drop in trust, and the shield is back up and locked.

Our world is full of people who have suffered pain and experiences we find hard to relate to. We never know who is hurting. Some of these people might just be our neighbors, family, and even long-time friends.

We live in a world of division and barriers of all kinds, getting in the way of connection.

Countless shields are up and secured tightly.

There is great risk in looking beyond the smile, the risk of losing what is comfortable, what is safe.

It could mean turning our own perspectives upside down.

It could mean yielding our own shields.

It could cost us vulnerability. It could cost us the relationship itself.

But I don't think our purpose is to skim the surface of friendships.

We are here to make a difference.

What if we set our hearts to do just that?

You never know what we might learn.

You never know what lies beneath.

Prone to Wander

Psalm 119: 175-176...the ending

"Invigorate my life so that I can praise you even more, and may your truth be my strength!

I'll never forget what you've taught me, Lord, but when I wander off and lose my way, come after me, for I am your beloved."

These verses are a perfect snapshot of who we are in real life.

On fire for God one minute...lost in the brambles the next.

We want oh-so-much to keep God close as we walk our own path but eventually for one reason or a thousand, we meander off and lose our way.

We ask for His truth to be our strength and then trust Him enough to ask Him to infuse vitality into our lives. We pray for vim and vigor.

And in exchange for all this, we make promises we can't keep.

Talk about a lop-sided relationship!

We become like Peter, and get all pumped-up-excited and vow that we will NEVER, EVER, EVER forget what He has taught us.

We fervently mean it when we say it. We really do.

But then like the psalmist, we find ourselves asking God to come after us, WHEN inevitably we wander.

The psalmist says WHEN because he knows he WILL wander and WILL lose his way. We are just like him. We are prone to wander.

In Robert Robinson's song from 1758, "Come Thou Fount", these universal words are found:

"Prone to wander, Lord, I feel it. Prone to leave the God I love."

"Here's my heart, oh take and seal it. Seal it for Thy courts above."

No matter where we wander, in all our trials, we can turn to Him...even in advance and as many times as we need.

Fortunately for us, He is the God of second chances.

He will take our bruised hearts and seal them with His love.

We have hope because we know WHO God is!

He is the God who will come and find us wherever we have gone, no matter if it is the depths of despair, the grime of the gutter, or the hiding place in our souls.

He will come for us. He will find us.

He always does.

Always.

And when we are at our lowest low and do not believe we deserve yet another rescue, He will breathe life into us.

He will invigorate us and fill us up!

He already knows our weaknesses…and he binds them in the sure & solid strength of His love.

He takes our mistakes as well as our very real sins and with his mighty hand throws them to the farthest corner from where we stand and says He will remember them no more. That is love, sweet and holy love.

Beloveds, we are loved by the almighty God!
He will come for us…rescue us.
And when He does, He will say…Come! Follow me.
For I will give you abundant life!

Every. Single. Time.

Go! Go Row That Boat!

Years ago, I dated someone who loved to sail. I loved the view. Seeing the sun set from the middle of a lake is magic. The gentle rocking of the boat, the whisper of the sails flapping in a breeze, the golden glow of the sky...those are memories I will never forget.

I loved those evenings on the lake! We would pack a picnic and sail out to the far north of the lake, enjoying the cooling breeze on a hot summer's night.

Spring sailing is much more wild than summer, with those big winds coming in gusts and calling for much maneuvering of sheets and managing the boom back and forth. Since my knowledge of sailing added up to a big zero, my only job was to manage a little rope in the middle of the boat called the Cunningham, which flattens the main sail for heavy winds, a fairly easy job for a non-sailor.

I needed to remember to duck my head under the boom when we tacked 45 degrees into the wind, zig zagging our way up the lake.

It looks deceptively easy from the shore, but sailing is a lot of work.

My date could read the wind better than anyone on that lake. He could manage his Flying Scot alone. That was a good thing because I never learned to sail. I never learned to sail because I never learned to swim.

One evening we had sailed north when the wind slowed to a breeze and then stopped. No leaves moving on the trees on the sides of the lake; no ripples in the water. Nothing. Hoover Reservoir is small compared to Lake Erie, but from its powerful dam to the farthest point north it is eight miles long and we were pretty far north when the wind stopped.

Loss of wind is not unusual. Wind is fickle and past excursions told me it would pick up soon. This time it didn't. Time passed. The sun set. The sky darkened. The gentle knocking of the boat that earlier mimicked the smoothest rocking chair, now felt a little threatening.

I enjoy walking along the ocean, or being close to lakes and rivers. But my fear of deep waters goes way back. As much as I loved being on that boat all the times we sailed, there was never a moment that I was not aware of the dangers of not being a swimmer.

So…I stopped the frightening mental tape of what lurked below, substituted a calming tape and wondered what our next steps might be. Eventually, I turned to him and asked, "what are our choices" and "what can I do to help?"

I own the fears I mentioned, but in a crisis, big or small, I get it together quickly. I can shove fear way down inside and do whatever needs to be done. I have lots of stories of crazy things I have powered through. If there is a crisis, I'm your person.

He looked around confirming lack of wind with no real potential for any to come and said, "We need to row back to shore." I looked down the lake, noting just how much rowing this was going to entail, turned to him and asked, "Which side do you want me on?"

We rowed and talked that night, sometimes silent with our own thoughts. We alternated quiet words with comfortable silence. We rowed till our arms were stiff and sore. We were young and in good shape so we stopped only to roll our shoulders every now and then.

In sailing you are in a position of one person in front of the other for much of the sail. But when you row, you row side by side the entire time, a completely different dynamic. You must time the dip of your paddle into and out of the water simultaneously with the other person.

You establish a rhythm and you have to keep that rhythm up continually. I liked gliding in the water and knowing we were powering this boat with the strength of our bodies and our minds. Our paddles worked WITH the water, not against it.

Being in perfect synch with someone is a beautiful thing.

I liked that I was doing my part and my part was now equal to his part and that felt good. Contributing to the solution was exhilarating. And it felt good to override my fear of water with a meaningful task.

It was pitch dark when we made it back to the docks. I was surprised that I didn't feel even a bit of weariness. Instead, I felt triumphant, capable, confident, proud.

Every time I hear the phrase, "When there is no wind... row!", I think of that night.

I think of that night and know that when life hands me a difficult problem, when I'm left with seemingly no possible solutions to a crisis, or untenable situation, I need to calm my breathing, push the fears aside, look toward the target and do the one thing I can do to move myself closer to the goal.

That method always works for me...always.

Life handed us a whopping crisis in 2020.

We felt there was no viable solution in sight. We will have other seemingly insurmountable difficulties that arise because we know that life, as wondrous as it is, holds many challenges.

For every challenge we face, we can assess the scenario in front of us and do the ONE thing that will move us forward and through.

One thing well done will take us miles ahead.

Daily I remind myself of this.

I have a choice. I can stay still in the water and watch night turn into day in the very same spot. Or I can pick up the paddle on my own side of the boat and row ... one dip at a time.

Some of us are fortunate to have someone to row with. Never underestimate the power of that connection and the depth of growth that occurs when we go through difficult times together.

Others are rowing alone. Even though we may be one person in one boat, we are at least in the same lake with others and can encourage each other from our own individual point of view.

Look around!

What is the ONE thing you CAN do that will move you forward?

When we feel like there is no wind in sight, go...go row that boat.

What Love Looks Like

On Valentine's Day and Beyond

To all my friends and family who are in beautiful marriages and wonderful relationships, God bless you!

You are shining examples of how love is supposed to look. You give hope and encouragement to so many people. Love on, dear ones!

To those who once had this kind of love and no longer have that honor, God bless you!

The respect and love you have shown them are an inspiration to others. You are not forgotten. And you are loved!

To those who would have given everything for this kind of love, despite having faithfully given it, God bless you!

And despite the fact that the world rarely recognizes your loss and rarely offers support, you are seen by an all-knowing God. And you are loved!

Finally, to those for whom the holiday brings sadness, feelings of being left out, lost and alone, please know that you are loved by the greatest lover of all...Almighty God!

He knows your every need and desire.

He seeks your heart, your life and your love.

He is the one true and faithful love!

And He knows we are our best when we reach out to others.

There is no better cure for loneliness than getting outside ourselves and focusing on others. The world provides many opportunities to do just that, especially now!

That's what love looks like too!

Love in Reflection

Love is a MIRROR of all you call dear, one to another and back again.

It is a reflection of the shimmer in your eyes to the depth of your lover's soul.

Love is your favorite piece of chocolate, melting at the warmth and spreading delight throughout your senses!

And Love is a lazy Sunday afternoon, when you eschew hard shoes, restrictive belts and uncomfortable wear for the quiet, sure presence of your favorite person, some bread, and perhaps some wine; maybe a book… but definitely a LOOK!

Love can be the greatest SYMPHONY ever played in perfect harmony and mesmerizing melodies with the inevitable clash of disconcerting dissonance thrown in for good measure.

Love is the greatest STORY ever told!

Surprise, Suspense, Speculation!

Hysterical encounters, misdeeds and missteps.

Passionate plots and playful transitions.

Captivating characters woven throughout enough character developments; thickening plots and thickening waists for a lifetime of intrigue and compelling endings.

Love is the cry in the night that says, "I need you" through unintelligible words and unimaginable sounds.

Love is the steepest hill with the most treacherous terrain, and hidden sites to stumble and fall—and yet it is the lifeline of hope that pulls you UP, and OUT, and ON...On to the top of the mountain, where the view is so worth the climb.

Love is the river that perpetually flows over the roughest rocks and makes them smooth.

Love is the steady beat of LIFE'S own metronome, that moves you from the impossible to the possible in perfect and imperfect timing.

Love is taking a first step and then another...away from the solitary, step by step... finding your footing again onto solid ground, to the one place you call HOME.

Love is the kindest WORD ever said that calms your soul and enlarges the realm of your understanding...of knowing!

Love is a LOOK, an endless look deep into the eyes of the one you know and the one who knows you well.

Yes, Love is a Mirror of all you call dear, one to another and back again.

You Are Who You Say You Are

You are...

The healer of my soul, the guardian of my bruised spirit.

You are the One who accepts who I am despite worldly rejections.

You are the One who dries my tears when no one sees they exist.

You hear my silent cries and know my deepest hurt.

You are the One who is there beside me when I dislike the things I see reflected from my soul.

You call my name and refute those hurtful words, the condescending conversations, the thoughts that destroy.

You are the One who whispers in my ear..."Go on", "Stand up", Stand firm".

You remind me of what is good in me that I cannot find and tell me it never went away.

You tell me it's ok to be misunderstood.

You tell me to wait for understanding and seek it in all the right places.

You tell me I am and will be loved...and the wait will be worth every empty moment.

You look at my repeated mistakes and tell me I have learned from every single one. You point out how.

You reach into my soul and choose the best and hold it as a mirror in place of what I choose to see.

You are the mighty redeemer of my soul!

You are the Rock on which I stand.

You are the reason I can stand and stand still amid a chaotic, whirling world.

You are the creator and conqueror of this world.

You are the purest love, never withheld, never bargained, never stained.

You are filled with tender mercies, cleansing forgiveness, freedom filled grace.

You are sure and true and constant.

You are exactly who you say you are and exactly who I need.

I will tell your story and live my life in grateful praise until I breathe my last..."You Are".

Light Always Comes

I woke up this morning at 4:30, a terrible, realistic nightmare sticking in my head. I put on my soft, cozy robe and started walking through my house to shake off the lingering fear.

Peering through the blinds, I saw pure, uninvaded snow on my deck, the shadow of the Christmas pine bouquet on my porch, and the bare branches of my beloved trees. I walked around the room, drank warm tea and milk, thought of my many blessings, prayed for the people on my list.

I went back to bed just as the first light was peeking through my blinds.

It's always light, isn't it, that pierces the darkness of our thoughts or our nightmares.

Light that brings comfort and peace and eventually joy.

So, fitting for Christmas...and for the third day of Christmastide.

Rest today and know that the One who brings us Light can pierce the darkest parts of our lives and our world, right now and whenever it is that we need Him.

Rest and know that Light always comes!

Part Two:

What We Learn from Joy

I Was Born in Love with Breezes

I'm happiest when I'm smack in the middle of a steady breeze. I delight in the feeling of my hair being wildly out of control and the air I'm breathing is as fresh as the newest dew on glistening grass.

I get lost in all of that. My mood shifts easily to bliss, and the agitations of this world fade into nothingness. How could I be out of sorts when an intoxicating breeze is dancing around my face. How could I be distraught with the world when I'm in the middle of a mighty wind and it feels magnificent to me.

If I can't be on top of a mountain then at least let me stand on a hilly knoll and be carried away by a gusty prevailing wind. And if I must be inside, then open all the windows. Even in the rain I ease the windows up to get a good cross breeze.

I can still see the frustrated look on the face of my long-suffering dad when he would tell my teenage self for the millionth time to "Close the window, Linda Beth. The furnace is on."

I need fresh air like I need words to read, music in my head, and ice water on an August afternoon.

It clears the pathways in my mind and blows the bad away.

And it has been known to be a remedy for fussy infant colic.

The story as told by my patient mom was that I cried a lot as an infant, probably colic, but who really knows with infants.

The only thing that would calm and quiet me in the wee hours of the night was fresh air, specifically, powerfully breezy fresh air.

We lived in a rental right beside the railroad tracks and it seems my favorite thing was being outside when a train would rumble by. As soon as I heard any sign of an incoming train, I would transform from all out, ear-piercing banshee to a smiling, giggling baby. I knew what was next. I was waiting for the wind!

Mama said as soon as the wind whooshed over my face, I would utter blissful baby sounds as if I had not just wakened the devil himself with my banshee screams. It was as if an internal switch were flipped and whatever plagued me was immediately put to rest. Eventually all those comforting railroad sounds and the powerful air it produced would lull me back to sleep and give my parents a much-needed break... until the next night.

Thank God for the B & O Railroad and those miraculous tracks that brought the breeze to a tiny baby in a tiny spot in West Virginia.

As I grew older my love of breezes grew with me.

One of the most magical places I have been in my adult life is on top of Middle Mountain In West Virginia.

I think of it as God's perfect combination for all manner of love...familial, platonic, and if you are really lucky, forever love.

There's nothing like lying on a blanket surrounded by the intoxicating scent of majestic pines, and feeling like you can reach out and touch the night sky. It's that close, full of stars and the wonders of the Milky Way.

The moon is showier on Middle Mountain. The air tingles with clean, top-of-the-mountain newness.

And the breeze...the breeze is pure, fresh, and enchanting.

If you're with the right person... you can't help but fall in love.

Forget the Fountain at Tiffany's...this is THE number one romantic place for me and it's all about the air.

I think if you took your troubles to that mountain and spent time on your knees with God, soft pine needles, and his purifying air, you would come away a different person. The breeze alone would clear your head and heal your heart.

I'm always looking for a cross breeze, ready for the wind to do its work and move the spirit inside of me. Sometimes I feel like a waterless wind surfer...poised to take the next wave of air, ready for anything.

To this day breezes bring me the promise of both peace and exhilaration. They have been God's gift to me for over 70 years now.

He has opened windows in the middle of winter all my life and given me moments of outlandish grandeur in the midst of chaos and turmoil.

I have conjured perfect peace with just the tiniest lifts of His wind and breezes. Holy Air…Holy Spirit! What sublime and mighty gifts!

And Yet, I Welcome Joy

It's 5:45 in the morning. I log roll over and dangle my feet over the edge of the bed.

My head hurts and those dangled feet ache. My neck is screaming for release of constant pain. My eyes are dry and yet unfocused. My hands feel like immovable clumps.

And despite elevating them all night, my legs are still swollen and painful.

These days I start each day with ever present pain and an unsteadiness that needs to wear off by moving forward despite the great urge to just lie back down.

Nausea follows me to the kitchen and tells me that nothing will sit well in my stomach quite yet.

The thought of coffee both entices and repulses me.

I begin my long list of morning stretches and feel the torn muscles of my shoulder expand with pain, as something clicks back into place. 4 months out from the fall that dislocated my shoulder, broke my nose, injured knees, and left me with a concussion…and still I hurt in every possible place. Adding this new thing to all the decades old "other things" has made me a little cranky this morning.

And what do I see first thing on my iPhone: "Be Happy! Don't Worry!"

Oh goodie! (Eye rolling) Sure.

Tell me again…how?

One big glass of water later and the coolness spreads throughout my body.

Stepping out onto my deck, I feel all the "things" begin to shift and slowly fade.

A few more minutes of stretching and moving my head around and letting my eyes land on my neighbor's magnolia tree and the roses underneath … my other neighbor's umbrella slightly swaying in the breeze and my mood lifts along with the fog from my brain.

I breathe in the summer's early air and I say out loud, just so I can hear myself think, "This is another morning that I am alive, another chance, another time to cherish the good and the bad, the fair and the unfair."

Be thankful you can stretch and move.

And in spite of myself, I smile.

Joy came to me all on its own by way of gratitude.

I laugh a little out loud at myself and look over to see my other neighbor, who is smiling and shaking his head at the crazy he sees, as I maneuver through my modified yoga moves.

I greet him and the new morning with a nod, ratted hair and all.

I give silent thanks for little things and welcome all the joy that may come my way today and I walk back inside, ready for that coffee now. And oh, yes, don't I have strawberries in my fridge too? What else is there?

And now I bow a humble "namaste" to my neighbor and say it out loud...Thank you, Lord, for this day.

"This is the day the Lord has made. Let us rejoice and be glad in it."

Psalm 118:24

Sleep Number TMI

If you know me even a little bit, you know that I believe in the adage "Knowledge is Power". The more information I have, the better I feel. I love details as much I do the visionary "big picture". Basically, I want it all.

When I discovered Google in the late 90's, I was ecstatic. Free Encyclopedias at my fingertips!

Ask me for help and I'll ask twenty questions to get a clearer perspective. I'm not a surface responder. I go in for the deep dive.

Ask me a question about your iPhone and I will offer several step-by-step suggestions. I'll only know the current one I'm using, but I will research your model and write a detailed response. I don't like loose ends.

I'm not fooled easily. I know the only reason I get these calls is that I am one thousand times more patient than most people's adult children after they have been texted a million times with the same question…in their defense.

I empathize…because I *am that parent*!

Just ask my children. They tend to tell the truth.

Do not mistake me for an expert on technology (I am literally "LOL-ing" at the irony of that sentence). My "help" on iPhones is limited to questions like these: "how to turn it off"; "how to turn it on"; "how to turn your flashlight off when you didn't mean to turn it on in the first place"; "how to delete your already deleted photos" (if I deleted it once, why must I delete AGAIN? One delete should suffice, Apple.)

And I admit that my helpful response for questions that go beyond this level is usually: "Turn your phone completely off, grab a cup of coffee/wine, do some yoga, or file your nails. Then turn it back on". It's the phone version of a TV "reboot". We all need a break sometimes, even our devices.

Once again, I have offered TMI. (that's Too Much Information, for you less hip folks). I recognize that saying "less hip" makes me anything but…and I acknowledge the irony.

Back to details... I love them.

So, when I got my Sleep Number bed, I was thrilled to find out that in addition to finding your "sweet spot" number, it also calculates the quality of sleep, in copious detail! Bingo!!! At last, I'm going to learn why I wake up exhausted.

I couldn't wait to get my morning report. The categories are: level of restful sleep, level of restless sleep, # of bed exits (Ha!), improvement options or "Atta-girl" comments.

There was just one problem... I never received a good score. Not one.

Turns out I stink at sleeping. This is really nothing new to me. Since my first child arrived in 1989, I have not slept well or long.

Before that I could fall asleep standing up at a live concert, leaning on my boyfriend's shoulder, or on my in-laws living room floor at a Friday night family dinner.

I once was a great sleeper, not necessarily a great date.

Things are sadly different now and I have the failing report cards to prove it.

You would think I would love all this detail. I did at first. I tried all their suggestions. I had motivation.

In all honesty, and great envy, I think this report of detailed, helpful sleep data was written by really brilliant and earnest 30-somethings, whose only fault was not being 60-something sleepers.

Waking up to a failing grade on a sleep report card every morning was depressing and demoralizing. I was downright despondent. Too bad I wasn't graded on "Use of Alliteration".

After weeks of trying all the suggestions and progressing to a measly 41% grade, I began to ignore the report. I figured I would be in my mid-70's before I could bring my grade up to passing.

Then, I had the brilliant idea to trick the bed's computer.

So, I started sleeping on the other side of the bed! I gave myself another name on the bed's register and started over. My alter ego, Linda Victoria, would have better grades than Linda Beth for certain. I went to bed smug, believing I could at least hit 50%! All I needed to do was: Stay in one position all night (movement equals restless sleep); Stop looking at the clock or my phone (how they know this is shocking and kind of creepy); Quit doing my stretching exercises in bed (Again: restless sleep); Limit my bed exits to 1 (right...HA!).

The next morning the report said: "There is no data on last night's sleep". The profile had not recognized Linda Victoria because I had not registered her. And if you are not registered, you are lost to their data! Wait! Bingo! Gotcha, Sleep Number!

I was hiding out from the Sleep Number police…in my OWN bed! That's just sad.

After a while, I realized that a good night's sleep for someone who gets the AARP magazine, just means not consuming caffeine after 4:00; not eating after 7:00; getting to bed by 9:00. All the things in all the articles.

I no longer look at the report…and that particular APP now hides on the last page of my iPhone. I exit the bed whenever I want to, do my stretching exercises in bed. My back and neck thank me for it. I'm blatantly sleeping on both sides of the bed and sometimes in the middle. This is as close as I get to living on the wild side.

It's truly a marvelous bed, the best bed I have ever had and I love sleeping in it!

Moral of the story: There is such a thing as "Too Much Information"!

Sometimes a little mystery is a good thing!

The Coffee Conundrum

This morning I stumbled into the kitchen around 4:30, no longer able to pretend I was sleeping. The thought of brewing some luscious coffee fueled my steps. And then I remembered that unfinished small cup of drive-through Tim's, purchased yesterday and placed in the fridge for the next coffee jag. I opened the refrigerator, but before I could secure the Tim's safely in my stiff hands, that cup of Joe jumped off the ledge and splattered everywhere, inside the fridge and out.

As I watched it seep under the fridge, panic set in. I like my coffee with lots of milk/cream and this cup was that perfect khaki color. You're familiar with the smell of spoiled milk, right? Hence, the panic.

There is no way, even 10 years ago, I could have moved that fridge on my own steam.

Yet, a full container of coffee was headed under it at the speed of light.

As quickly as a cranky, sleep deprived person can "hop to it", that's the speed I summoned to clean up this mess.

A half roll of paper towels later (heartfelt apologies to minimalists and tree lovers, of which I am the fan club president), the coffee was still pouring from some unknown place. But where?

I had sopped up the 3 shelves it dripped down from; the wine, cheese and chocolate middle drawer; the pull-out freezer, and of course the floor.

Surely, there was no more coffee left to clean up! But there it was, annoyingly appearing again in all the places I had just cleaned. I retraced my steps and pulled out drawers and shelves to see if it had pooled inside those areas. Nope! It had not!

I did the final clean up with sterner stuff, mopped the floor, wrung out my rags for the zillionth time, straightened my very twisted body, & decided ironically to make myself a hot cup of the devil the right way!

I turned on the gas under my humble pour over coffee pot, turned around, and turned red. Coffee was pooling again on the floor and dripping all over the parts I had scoured minutes ago.

Where in the world was this coming from? I jerked open the doors, not too lovingly, I might add, expecting to see the culvert culprit staring me in the face. But...Nothing.

Still, coffee relentlessly dripped. Now my annoyance transformed into curiosity. I was on a mission.

I took most everything out of my fridge and freezer. All 4 of my brothers-in-law are shaking their heads right now. They know, along with anyone who has ever stepped foot in my kitchen, this is no small task. What in the world was going on? Fridge Monster, "Show Yourself"!

Was this payback for all the many times I have admonished my fridge for its wrongdoings, especially the Ice Maker? Surely the Ice Maker was involved in these shenanigans!

Was I slowly slipping to the other side of sanity? I'll never know!

I'm keeping watch from a chair by the fridge, until "rational me" takes over and sings "Let it go! Let it go!" For the sake of sanity, some mysteries are best left unsolved.

This morning both my Samsung ice maker and my Keurig coffee maker sounded like an 80-year-old woman in a tractor pull contest.

Such grunting and explosive cacophony I have not heard since I tried to get out of bed the day after my knee replacements.

I know these things don't last forever, but my Keurig is just 9 years old and the ice maker is a mere 6 years old.

Surely in appliance years, those are babies, right?

I feel like a tyrant every time I ask either of them to do their thing.

I drink a whole lot of ice water throughout the day and I'm getting a big case of "ice guilt".

And it doesn't help that the dials on my Keurig look like they are in a constant stage of this...

With my coffee maker it is a continual, gravelly, choking sound that makes my neck hurt just listening to it. RRR.. RRR...RRR...

Poor thing!!

I find myself speaking encouragingly... "Just a little bit more water and you're almost there!"

I feel a little less empathy toward the ice maker as I have to defrost it every two weeks by way of a portable steamer (recommended to me by the one and only appliance repair person who will even touch my particular refrigerator.)

The noises from my ice maker come in two stages...first a really long and painfully, difficult burp as it is gearing up and then 4 minutes later as it dumps the last two cubes, it sounds like a sickly wheezing old man's cough.

It's no wonder I always look closely at those ice cubes before I take a big drink.

Lest you think I have a kitchen-full of doomed appliances, let me assure you that I still have my Magic Microwave that always returns the handle of my coffee cup to the front (this is a short person's dream coffee cup position) as long as you key in the time for any number that ends in 7... 7 seconds, 17 seconds, 27 seconds... you get the idea.

My Magic Microwave brings me great joy every single morning!!! And many times throughout the day...and into the night if I'm drinking hot water for a winter's sore throat.

It is THE BEST GE Microwave a short person could EVER want!!!

So there!

Don't cry for me, Facebook-tina!!!
The truth is, I'll never leave you...
Just don't make trouble!

Let's talk garbage disposers. Why not.

Definition of Garbage Disposer from the Floyd-Huling Practical LifeSkills Unabridged Dictionary:

"A noisy mechanism in your kitchen sink, whose purpose is to grind up food to tiny bits and suck them down a disposal system that magically takes them far away from your sight and smell, thus making your cooking life so very easy and joyful".

We all know it doesn't exactly work like that, mainly because humans tend to ignore owner's manuals of just about everything mechanical.

PRACTICAL TIPS for this Nirvana: Read the owner's manual.

There are some basic things you should know if you are going to use one of these.

Things you should not put in garbage disposers: bones, coffee grounds, eggshells, plastics, wooden spoons, metal spoons, marbles, nails, screws, etc. I'm adding the "etc." because humans can surprise you with the stuff they shove down those drains and naively think will be swept away into nothingness without a hitch or a screech!

A seasoned garbage disposer repairman once told me he retrieved a broken hairbrush and comb from a customer's garbage drain. Now, a wooden spatula I understand; a tiny plastic funnel I get; even children's toys I understand. But a hairbrush and comb…just can't picture what led up to that one!

This is what you get when you leave the owner's manual in its original plastic covering or you throw it away entirely, all righteous, because you 'live in a paperless society now'.

All that aside, let's say you truly are "homeowner of the year" material and you put in your disposer only what is allowed by the powers that be. Still, you can get into big trouble.

We'll talk later about "big trouble" but first I must ask this important question:

Do you clean your disposer, and if so, HOW do you clean it? Do you use those little paper packets of charcoal, malic acid, and sodium laurel sulfate? That stuff is so strong that it will ruin your eyes and skin if it comes in contact with them. (That's why they say: Do Not Open Packet) Instead, you just stuff them down the disposer with great confidence, like you are committing a disposer felony on purpose. Since you've read the label of all that toxic stuff, you figure that some super amazing cleaning will be going on in that drain and you feel confident that you have done the right thing.

You get the water just so hot, then pencil thin, then stuff that packet down. The screeching begins and remains until you mercifully see the blue bubbles receding.

Even after all that has gone on and you have flushed a gallon of good water down the drain to flush out the toxins, have you ever checked to see if it worked? Do you even know what is stuck under those black, rubbery disposer flaps? Have you ever shined a light on "what lies below" or taken a paper towel to wipe up the tiny bit that might be left behind?

I have taken paper towels and wiped around the underside of those flaps and been absolutely disgusted with what ended up on my towels. The stinkiest, slimiest of black gunk! The stench of which practically knocks you out! No matter how horrific this always is, I cannot help myself from going at it over and over again. I am not satisfied until my towel comes out clean. And that takes forever and quite a lot of paper towels.

If you have discovered ANY of the above, I guarantee that you will no longer rely on sodium laurel sulfate to do ANYTHING helpful in your disposer!

Once I discovered this terrible truth about disposer cleaners, I decided to forego the packets of many names and just "do it myself". It has become a mandatory weekly chore. Once I'm finished, I do a little victory dance and quickly sterilize my hands in bleach.

So...back to "big trouble" ... One day a while ago I had the occasion to call the disposer repair guy about yet another garbage problem. He came out, fixed the drain and then waxed practically, if not poetically about garbage disposers, their function and their foibles. One question led to the next and what I learned from him downright astounded me! This was the same repairman who told me the "hairbrush/comb" story along with other harrowing things I will not repeat, especially if you are cooking right now.

But he said something at the end that shook my world.

He was very politely schooling me on why I should not put even **tiny bits** of food down the disposer, when I looked at him with a puzzled expression. Thinking there must be a funny punch line to this joke, I asked him why. He said that eventually I would just have to call him to come back and fix everything all over again. What? This was no joke.

I couldn't believe it, so the following conversation ensued:

ME: (Feeling somewhat confused)

"Now, I know not to put eggshells or bones or coffee grounds down the disposer, but now you are saying I can't put fish and chicken down there. So, what CAN I put down my disposer?"

HIM: "Nothing!"

ME: WHAT?

HIM: (Graciously repeating himself)

"NOTHING!"

ME: (Ramping up and pointing to my sink's disposer opening)

"It says right here on this disposer: FOOD WASTE DISPOSER"!

Him: "I know."

ME: "Then why do we have them at all?"

HIM: (nodding his head sagely)

"Exactly."

ME: (Stupidly persisting)

"I'm serious…what can I put down the disposer?"

HIM: (Looking at me kind of sadly and maybe with a touch of disappointment at my apparent dullness)

"Nothing! Do. Not. Put. Anything. Down there!"

HIM again: (Pausing for emphasis)

"I've been in this business almost 30 years and I have found that disposers were not made to handle all that junk.

ME: (Too loudly) "Then what WERE they made for?"

HIM: (With supernatural patience)

"Ma'am, you can do what you want, but **Nothing good comes from putting garbage down that drain!"**

ME: (Still shocked, but with the dawning of what this would mean from here on out; also knowing I had pushed him far enough), I sadly exclaimed...

"Well! Good grief!"

And with that brilliant response, I thanked him for his work and his wisdom and paid that very patient man.

I walked him to the door, then sat down to properly mourn the loss of my favorite kitchen cleanup toy.

ONE YEAR LATER: Only liquids and near-liquid stuff are allowed to enter my disposer now, overlooking the occasional errant, cheating behavior.

Mostly I heed that man's advice.

I am not recommending this policy for you.

If your disposer has been faithful to you, I applaud it and wish you well.

You know what they say: Garbage in, Garbage out!

Garbage In, Garbage Out...Reprisal

(The Lessons Learned Version)

Life Lessons Learned from the Kitchen:

* You have heard this one all your life!
Garbage in, garbage out!

If we put garbage into our souls, our minds and in our words, we can't expect to produce shining acts or speak pearls of wisdom.

* If we shine a light on the deep, dark place where we stuff all the garbage of our lives, we might find some rotten thinking and some rotten behaviors. We can't just leave it there and try

to cover it up or flush it out. It's not going away without some serious deep cleaning.

* There are no miracle packets! We have to DIY it all the way!!

We can't rely on someone else or something else to do the really tough jobs in our lives. We are the best choice to do that hard work. We will have to roll up our sleeves, get our hands dirty, and do the hard work all by ourselves.

* If we want to clean up the mess the right way, we can't fight toxic with more toxic.

We need to pour light into that darkness. We need to find different ways to speak. We need to speak the truth, not lies. We need to be kind, patient, loving, even when there is dirt all around us. We need to persevere through the messy parts and know that life is full of messy parts. We need to accept that nothing will be perfect, but all of it can be for good.

* Don't put anything dirty down that drain!
* We need to be mindful of what we feed our brains, our thoughts, our hearts.
* Clean thinking means good, positive, wholesome, healthy, thinking.
* We will never regret the discipline it takes.

* In the end a clean slate is definitely worth it!
In the end you will feel triumphant. You might even do a victory dance!

And last, this is an ongoing job! We don't stay shined up for very long.

Real world living calls for real world cleaning!
It's good!
It's healthy!
And it smells good too!

"The light shines in the darkness, and the darkness has not overcome it." John 1:5

"Your word is a lamp for my feet, and a light on my path." Psalm 119:105

"For what has been stored up in your hearts will be heard in the overflow of your words." Matthew 12:34

Unapologetic Bird Eavesdropper!

I'm an unapologetic bird eavesdropper!

I like to imagine dramatic romances played out on the rooftops and treetops all around my neighborhood.

I have heard more than an ear-full in my own back yard.

Sipping coffee on my deck, waiting for the sunrise, I hear the high trill of the red-winged blackbird, as he preens and dips into the nearby fountain. If I wait till the sun has cleared the pines, I can hear the soprano arias of the yellow warblers, encouraging their young, as they make their way to a breakfast fit for baby champions...juicy garden worms.

All day long I hear the song thrush as he sings from dawn till dusk. I think of him as the conversant mayor of Migratory Alley, with his suit of cream and brown. His constant chatter and stylish coat of upside-down hearts tickles my fancy.

Much later as the sun travels low in the west, I hear the plaintiff calls of the whip-poor-wills.

I'm drawn into sadness by the repetitive 4-note song of the mourning doves.

I hear cardinals call out to other cardinals as they wait for the tentative responses of their would-be mates.

Every now and then I spot aerial playmates gracefully dancing on air. They tumble and twirl, dip and soar and bravely stick the landing on the branches in my maple tree every time.

If only I spoke sparrow, or finch, cardinal or wren I would know their stories for sure.

I need to learn the language of finches, blue birds, prothonotary warblers and red bellied woodpeckers because their non-stop chatter reminds me of neighborhood busy bodies as they flit from one place to another spreading the news, endlessly building nests.

Time disappears when I step out on my deck.

Looking through the lens of my binoculars, I feel like a voyeur on my own porch.

Close your eyes and listen…

With a little imagination and a bit of patience, you can enter the world of birdsong.

There's entertainment in the air: morning songs, evening love notes, mingling migration buddies and imagined liaisons.

As long as I can step onto my deck, or into the woods, I'll be listening in, eavesdropping on the greatest concert in town.

Little Buddy

I've called him Little Buddy since I first spotted him on my deck one fine spring evening a few years ago.

It was getting to be dusk, that magical time just after sunset and well before the sky deepens to navy, and readies itself for the nightly star show.

The sky was a lovely light blue with cottage cheese clouds and a hint of a breeze.

He was sideways on my siding, hanging on for dear life, medium-light green and splayed flat. He was the cutest, most tenacious tree frog I had ever seen.

I walked closely to him and spoke softly in his direction, hoping not to frighten him enough to fall off his precarious clutch on the cream vinyl of my walls.

He stilled his movements and hung on motionless for an hour.

I went back to my own perch in my wrought iron chair by my computer and continued to write, eventually forgetting about him as I edited my way to the finish of a tricky passage.

As the sky darkened, I looked up and he was gone. I figured he was merely passing through on his way to a tree frog convention.

The next evening, as I was grilling a late supper of veggies and fish, I saw him again, this time catching bugs by my lone light on the wall.

I greeted him with "Hello, Little Buddy, are you lost or have you come to stay?"

This time I knew better than to walk toward him. I kept busy turning peppers, potatoes and pieces of cod.

When I turned again, I caught a glimpse of him sneaking into the large blue pot that held my tallest Majesty Palm.

So that is where he slept last night! I imagined him burrowed in the soil and blanketed with little pieces of pine cone I had spread over the roots of that mighty palm. It would be a safe place from predators and dry from the elements but outfitted with a tray underneath to hold the excess water. It was going to rain that night and it felt right knowing he was going to be fine till the morning, with his tummy full of assorted bugs, hopefully a mosquito or two among them.

This could be a mutually beneficial relationship, my buddy and I.

As spring turned to summer, I would expect to see his wiry, little green body each evening, as he ventured closer and closer to where I would sit. One evening, engrossed in writing, I leaned back into the wrought iron rocker to rest my back, and almost squashed the little guy. He had been hanging on to the sides of my iron chair, a little too close for comfort...his specifically.

He jumped 4 feet away from my chair as I tried to console and convince him I didn't know he was there.

He took to hanging on my chair every evening, and sometimes it even looked like he was peering at the words on my screen.

Such an odd couple…my little buddy and me.

I'm quite fond of him, especially since we have the same initials, LB (Linda Beth and Little Buddy).

It felt like we both resided at the same address, two single beings, I lived inside and he on the Palm townhome. The next evening, I had bestowed upon me such an honor that tears came to my eyes when I saw him approach. Buddy in his light green outfit, and what might have been his partner and 2 mini "buddies" behind them. They inched slowly from the base of the Majesty Palm and traveled in the direction of my chair.

I held my breath. I really wanted to take a sip of my drink but did not dare do anything other than breathe.

So, here I am nervously watching this little family of tree frogs, coming to meet me. What language can I use? I have only one.

So, I quietly told him I was grateful to meet his family and I hoped they were comfortable in their home on Majesty Palm Lane.

I began to leave a flat bowl of water, no deeper than an inch, near the base of the palm. Just in case they would prefer a pool for the summer.

I asked where they would go for the winter but they just stared bug-eyed at me, probably thinking I was the dimmest human they knew. Dim but peaceful and harmless.

I saw them again the next spring, but without their offspring.

Finally, this spring and summer it took Little Buddy a long time to show up and show his face.

He looked sad to me. He was alone. I waited for his partner and maybe some new little ones to arrive, but so far just LB.

It's mid-August so I would have seen the rest of the crew by now if they were bunking in the Majesty Palm.

I could just be a dotty old lady, but I really do believe that Little Buddy and I have a friendship of sorts. At least we have a mutual understanding that both of us can live and exist happily on the same platform. We don't have to dominate each other. And we can peacefully share space without too many grievances.

Although I have to say, I got concerned when I found him 10 feet above ground on top of the outside of my bent outdoor umbrella. He must have taken a nap in the folds when it was closed and tied together…then was lifted when I opened up the umbrella that morning. That must have been a big surprise.

But I have seen him jump and if anyone can make it off that 10-foot umbrella it is Little Buddy! Now if I can just train him to "potty" in the plant and not on the umbrella, we'll be good!

It's June 1, and like clockwork, my pale green family guy is back, exploring his summer deck home, looking for the planter that is just right for his family.

He still has a long journey till he gets to the next Majesty Palm.

Sometimes they sleep on the screen of my sliding glass door, sometimes they hang out (literally) on the wrought iron chair I'm sitting in... always wherever I'm sitting.

Kind of endearing... kind of creepy!

They remind me to tread softly, carefully, responsibly mindful of my surroundings.

That's not a bad lesson as we continue to learn how to share our planet with each other.

Happy first day of June to you all!

May your journey today be safe and wise.

'Twas The Day Before Thanksgiving

'Twas the day before Thanksgiving and all through my fridge
Not a space was forthcoming, not even a smidge.

Pans of stuffing, nay dressing were lined in a row.
Did I really need two? That second must go!

This calls for emergency tactics galore!
Why did I wait till the Wednesday before?

Now lunching on celery, & whatever was in the jar on the left.
Still not going to make it and feeling bereft.

How many cartons of yogurt does one person need?
There's plain, blueberry and homemade, indeed!

I'm spotting bad habits; obsessions with cheese.

Good grief! There's the broccoli from last Halloween!

There's nothing to do but remove and start over,
Where IS Marie Kondo when I need a do-over?

The veggies, all regal and smug in their bins,
Were feeling sublime next to carb-laden sins.

The berries, how sweet, perfect healthy equations,
But why did I fall for the BOGO persuasion?

Now placing a side where once lettuce was lain,
I'm secretly cheering the demise of romaine.

At last, thank the stars, I found enough space
To save turkey and stock from utter disgrace.

At peace with the fridge and its well-stuffed sight!
Happy Thanksgiving to all, and to all a good night!

The Rumble in the Basement

It must have been the rumble to beat all rumbles!

Heads rolled! Literally!

Sixteen Weary Warriors, most of them "long in the tooth" (pun most definitely intended), fought fiercely in my basement these past 11 months. I'm talking about my Nutcrackers, of course.

I don't know what happens down there in those boxes, but it isn't pretty. Every year there are injuries, but this year was particularly brutal. Today I reattached a battle-weary helmet, a sword, a shoe, a drum, two broken noses, and an entire head! And the trim on one of the King's robes...and this was the Peaceful King, not the Warrior King!

Well, what should I expect?

They're not *really* "cute" are they? Look at them close-ly and they are actually frightening, especially when their mouths are open, in "nutcracker" mode! I had to get rid of one once because he was just too scary. He was a Santa Claus Nutcracker! Imagine…Santa Claus with overly large teeth, looking lean and mean! No amount of fuzzy white beard could compensate for that image. He gave me the willies as I sipped eggnog alone one night. It might have been the eggnog, but still…

I bought my first one at CVS for $3.99, December, 1988 when I was pregnant with my first born, Jared. Three have been presents from friends. One Rocking Horse Nutcracker was given to my daughter, Kathryn, because she's crazy about horses. One came from Germany. Classy guy with real fur hair, but he doesn't seem to lord it over the others. They all seem to get along really well on the mantel above the fireplace.

So, what gives in the basement the rest of the year?

All I know is, I'm armed with my trusty glue gun when they emerge from those boxes.

They stand at the ready on the mantel. Winter Warriors ready and a little too willing to do battle! Gotta love those guys!

Hamilton Road Olympics

You all may not know this, but nearby Hamilton Road has qualified for the 2021 Summer-Fall-and most likely Winter Olympics in a category called Insanity Driving with OB and CCRAB (Orange Barrels) and (Confusing, Curvy Round-A-Bouts).

Complete with a 5-mile stretch involving high volume traffic from 5 lanes cut down to 2 and sometimes 1, peppered with unexpected and constantly changing cross over Orange Barrels that rival the LA highway enigma. This is an intense, reflex challenging course, not intended for the weak hearted.

The course is designed with 6 consecutive round-a-bouts, whose sharp curves induce vertigo & nausea, followed by the confusing, ever-changing orange barrel part of the course.

Competition is held both at Friday morning rush hour and Friday night restaurant scramble time. This is the multiple headlight blinding version.

I entered both competitions and I don't want to brag, but I gold-medaled that thing in record time this morning.

Don't mess with old folks with a 50-year advantage of vertigo driving skills. Also, I am a WV Country Roads Scholar, so...you know...curves mean nothing to me, babe!

I'll be competing in the nighttime version tonight, just in case you want to tune in.

I'm going for the Gold again...the Buckeye Senior Gold Card version!

Things I've Learned Since I Passed 70 & Did Not Collect $200

- You're one step away from a fall.
- Look down before you take that one step.
- The last part of "Look before you Leap" is a debatable concept.
- "Everything hurts" is status quo.
- The phrase "Everything hurts" is no longer funny.
- Nothing is the "new black" anymore.

- And that “little black dress” is now just that “black dress”.

- Sometimes the diagnosis alone can give you a panic attack.

- They need to make Prosecco bottles easier to open.

- Write down a list of Prosecco brands you can actually open by yourself. Tape it to the Fridge.

- Kirkland Signature is NOT one of them.

- Things taste different, but sugar is always there for you.

- Things smell different…maybe even you?

- Someone removed salt from the pantry.

- Were your kids just near your pantry?

- Daily showers are still necessary, just for different reasons.

- ‘Wake up and smell the roses’…can be easily shortened to ‘Wake Up’ and not change the inherent meaning.

- The “Hot Flashes” that were supposed to go away once you reached zero estrogen 20 years ago, are still there and still just as annoying.

- Sarcasm sadly comes more easily.
- "Think Before you Speak" is now written on a post it note and lives permanently on your fridge and on your dashboard.
- Yes, you have told that story before!
- No, no one wants to hear it again!
- Seriously, they don't.
- Referencing computers as CRTS is a conversation stopper.
- Changing your parent's "In my day" phrase to "It wasn't that long ago that…" has the same effect as "In my day" did 50 years ago.
- As soon as you are comfortable with a social media choice, the young ones move on. It's the fastest you'll see them move in your lifetime.
- You find yourself at that "in between stage" where dinner at 8:00 sounds like guaranteed GERD and dinner at 4:00 sounds like a 50% off milk shake.
- Is Hollywood Squares still a thing?
- It should be.

- It's hard to get a book published, but pretty much anyone can make a music video and "Go Viral" ... Anyone.

- No one seems to understand that "Go Viral" is a terrible term!

- The irony of having 7 different "universal" remotes has not affected any change.

- Good grammar should outlive us all!

- As you pass 70, you might lose your glasses, your patience, and even your sense of direction, but never lose your sense of humor.

Party of Two, Please

I love a party!

Notice I did not say I love TO party.

That tiny word makes all the difference in the world.

Hear me out on this.

I love the festive air of people gathering.

When I was young, I felt awkward at the beginnings of parties. I didn't quite know what to do with myself, or my hands, or where to walk, what group to join. I remember one pretentious corporate party where I spent an inordinate amount of time in the gilded bathroom, wishing I had brought a book.

All those years of thinking that everyone was looking at me, scrutinizing every move, and now I realize they were just looking for the party trays...looking for the good stuff.

Now at this well-earned "chill" stage of my life, I love those beginnings.

I love the sweet anticipation of it all. You can feel hope in the atmosphere, joy waiting to explode, like a little girl's giggle held too long in church.

If you have centered your Zen and your radar is dialed up to 10, you can even discern the longing for belonging in between all those other sensations.

If you stand still and close your eyes you can hear the many varied songs of laughter. You can hear the glasses clinking, the beverages being poured, the whisk of clothing as people gravitate to their spots, and the whoosh of air as they settle in.

In my family we love appreciative food sounds too…the "ummm" and the "yum"; the "wow", and the "oh, my gosh, have you tried this one yet?"

Best of all I love the low hum of conversation percolating in the different groups. Each group takes on a personality for as long as it is a group. In the best of parties, people mingle and change groups throughout the night, getting to know those different personalities better.

I do so love a party!

With all this gush about parties, you would think I might be the "Life of the Party" girl.

Oh, No! I am anything but that!

I do love to watch and listen to those charming folks, though. They mesmerize me. And they're fun.

I cheer them on, but I'm not one of them.

And I love the folks who can "work the party" as we used to say in corporate America. I say that "tongue in cheek" because these are truly gifted drifters. Over the course of the night, they will have checked in with each and every group, contributing to the conversations of all of them, delighting with their wit, their banter, their knowledge of so many different things. And then they glide out and on to another group. I am in awe of them.

But I'm not one of these either.

In the beginning I move in observation mode, take my time, and enjoy myself as I meander, having little chats here and there, and absorb the good vibrations of the party, until I find a group to join. And then I settle in and immerse myself completely.

At any given time, raucous laughter can be heard, or lots of leaning in to get every word someone is saying amid interesting and intense facial expressions. At this point of total immersion, I am completely unaware of party trays or any other distractions. It's the conversation that I care about.

Conversations are treasured gems to me, like the discovery that two of you love word games and dancing to jazz, or when you learn of a new method to teach early childhood reading. And then there's the conversation where you find someone who cares about the homeless as much as you do. Conversations like these are the source of new ideas and the foundations of good relationships.

If it's family or people who feel like family, then you'll also find me in the big, huggy groups. Those groups are the heartbeat of vibrant parties. This is where the story telling happens and the new stories are born. I want to be there, present for it all!

My specialty, though, is the party of two or three. That's where the deep dive conversations are taking place. It doesn't matter the topic, I am in for those conversations any time, any day, or any late night. And if they are taking place outside, staring at the heavens too, I am in my happy place.

I'm not any good at "chit-chat". I wish I were, but I can only last about 30 seconds.

After that, I'm all in for the story, the funny one, the heartfelt one, the 4 tissue one, the heartbeat alarm one, even the passionate fiery one where you lovingly discuss the pros and cons of, well...just about anything. That's where my heart lies. That's where my personality comes alive.

I crave the natural dynamics that ebb and flow. I love when people speak and pause...sometimes for effect...and sometimes just to let someone else in. When we don't come up for air, is when we lose that golden opportunity to hear someone else speak, to listen to what they bring to the table.

This is the absolute Zen of Party Talk.

Every one of these conversations remind me of our personal conversations with God.

For example, was there a time when you felt awkward starting a conversation with God...praying?

He's not looking for a formal speech or to scrutinize our every word. He is looking for the party trays...the good stuff in us.

Do we wake up our senses as we approach our prayer time with Him? Do we carve a special space or time for Him?

Do we view Him as "family" and give Him our tender truths, our real stories?

Do we completely immerse ourselves in those conversations?

Do we offer chit chat when He might want more? How do we get to the place of calm, a sense of belonging and an ease in beginning our time with Him?

If we decide to "deep-6 the chit chat" and deepen our relationship with Him, we'll need to disclose the whole truth and nothing but the raw truth about where we are at that very moment.

If we hide in the bathroom, we will lose the opportunity to find out more about Him and ourselves, what He has in mind for us and our future.

When we listen more than we talk, we create the space to hear and to grow each time we gather with Him.

We need to pause to hear Him and let His words sink in. And then we need to pause to let Him in to our hearts and in to our lives.

Pouring out our hearts to Him will feel like new life to us.

Listen closely and you can hear the sounds of love, grace, and mercy mingling between your soul and God, the real Life of the Party.

You can feel true belonging in this holy group...God and you.

It's the perfect party of two!

A Safe Place

I spent the morning with six women in the summer of 2021. Six very unique and intriguing women! We were missing two, one who was in Minnesota helping her son move into his new apartment. We missed her joy and her animated conversation. The second one was tucked in bed at home, sick. We missed her kind heart and her wisdom.

Eight has been our number for over nineteen years and we are best when we are all present and firing all our engines. Lori, Jeanne, Mary, Nancy, Helen, Linda W, Sandy, and I.

For the first 16 months of Covid, we had been zooming almost every 2 weeks, until 6 of the 8 of us were getting together in the same space at the start of summer.

Giddy with excitement and the opportunity to connect on an "up close & personal" level, we unashamedly stood in the middle of the street and greeted each arrival as if she were our long-lost cousin from Outer Slobovia.

It was a gorgeous day in Ohio, and we enjoyed the delights of a lush, magical backyard retreat. Fresh air and fresh ideas...who doesn't love that! Creativity abounds in this group of multi-age, multi-lingual, multi-background women and no one is *ever* at a loss for words.

After long hugs and exclamations of "Look at you!" wound down, we found our places outside under 3 cabana umbrellas. All gates were open as we immediately ping-ponged our way through the opening topic, which was how emotional we all felt finally seeing each other in person, how important eye contact and facial expressions were to connection and understanding, and the increased success of our Porch Fairy surprises. That led to the new Monet Art exhibit, which led us to our children and what new jobs, projects, and research they were involved with. This was a natural segue to discussions about parenting adult children and all the nuances that brings, and funny stories of grandparenting. At some point after lunch, we discussed the need for leadership and "buy in" from the top in order for any new program or product or workplace culture change to be successful. And that led to the need to promote education in skilled trades like electricians, plumbers, computer experts. And always the question is asked before our time ends, what books are you reading? And what are you doing for your well-being?

One idea follows another, sparking new tangents, nothing unusual for this group.

It happens every time we gather. This time seemed even more meaningful as we now knew what it was like to harness all this energy through electronic highways for 16 months.

I should pause here and say that we harnessed Zoom in exceedingly creative ways. We brought music, meditation, yoga, and art into our time slots, and learned to "share" screens & record special meetings.We celebrated milestone birthdays in high style right there in our Hollywood Squares Zoom. Humility aside, we bossed that Zoom Boom all over the place.

But "there's nothing like the real thing, baby"!

And breaking bread in the same shared space is the actual Bomb!

So, we listened carefully that day to what was said and what was not said.

We watched the eyes and faces of those around us like we were monitoring the first landing on the moon.

We were in active caring mode, something we excel in.

As the sun meandered to high noon, we began to reflect about the nature of our early morning discussion, how we loved our openness, the awareness that people were really listening to understand and not judge.

We talked about how conversations this open could easily go awry in certain scenarios.

I commented how wonderful it was to feel "safe" in conversation in this "oh-so-unsafe" world.

And then Mary remarked that we have been able to do this since the very first time we joined as a circle of caring women, all those years ago. We didn't know each other well then. But we began our first circle recognizing and believing that those present had real gifts to share.

That premise became our automatic stance: implied faith, immediate respect, with an open eye toward grace.

How rare! And how wonderful!

Grace and implied worth work so well in friendships. They are game changers in group dynamics.

In your life do you know the feeling of being able to say what you think, and express how you feel without being criticized, judged, or ignored?

Have you experienced the rare situation of finding a level of comfortability being exactly yourself in every way, in word choices, gestures, wide ranges of emotions, wide spectrums of interests, viewpoints, and perspectives, in your highs and in your lows?

Do you have a safe place to be you, completely you?

My buddy, the Google online dictionary, defines "safe" as "protected or not exposed to danger or risk; not likely to be harmed or lost."

That's exactly how we *should* feel among close friends and family.

If you can find even one person who guards your heart as you bare your soul, you have hit the jackpot.

If you can find more than one, you are living the dream.

And if you can find an entire group where this consistently happens, every single time you gather together...well, you have reached for the stars and touched one!

In my life I have found friends and close family members who are this safe, creative place for me, where I can be the unedited and mask-less me.They are the network of individuals who add value, joy, meaning, and love to my life. They keep me sane and they keep me centered. We keep our friendships alive through making space for each other. I am grateful beyond measure.

I do not take this gift lightly.

When you are given something so rare, then you want to offer it to others, to be that Safe Place for someone else. It's a win-win. It will deepen your relationships, widen your ability to empathize, and increase your joy!

It will give you one of life's greatest Super Powers...The ability to form true connections.

As for the group of women I mentioned at the start of this piece, we had yet another gathering later that month. This time rain was pouring in all directions and giant umbrellas offered no help at all, but nothing, absolutely nothing dampened our spirits!

As the rain pelted the front porch roof above us, we shook off our wet, squeaky shoes, and dived into the good food Mary had prepared, keeping up with the watercolor expressions and discussions that stimulated our brains and generated more questions.

In short, we stretched our comfort zones, went out on precarious limbs, and felt the sure comfort of being safe & real, just like always, rain or shine.

I wish you the same.

(Dedicated to the Goddesses from the heart of Hanby, established 2003, the Firepit YaYa's, established 2008, and to all of the incredible women and men in my life who excel at the Connection Super Power.)

Clearing Away

It always surprises me how much better I feel when my countertops are cleared away and down to the essentials, which include my canisters, a beautiful bowl, a small basket woven for me by a good friend, a tiny vase, and 4 depression glass coasters I have had since 1979.

These "essentials" bring me joy. Aside from the baking ingredients inside my canisters, the rest of the things are essential only to my soul. I like the way looking at them makes me feel, but I want a lot of space in-between them to feel at peace. I need peace.

Heritage, humble beginnings, friendship, family, beauty…it's good to be reminded of those things every morning when I take a moment to absorb whatever thoughts are slowly emerging from my brain.

Other items like candles I'm drawn to, a working grocery list, library books, or a recipe I'm making are the extra life props on my countertops. They live there in rotation for a while, but never permanently.

You could say the state of my countertops is a window to the state of my mind.

Clutter = chaos for me.

When I systematically remove, rearrange, or deep six the clutter, it feels like I'm also processing the chaos in my mind.

The pandemic brought a different kind of clutter into our homes and into our lives.

The very real symbols of that global mess have taken up space in selected corners of our homes.

Lysol wipes, 90% rubbing alcohol, various masks in zip lock bags, a digital thermometer, a lifesaving oximeter, and all the vitamins known to man...bulky pieces that occupy too much room in our homes and in our minds.

For two wonderful weeks I pared these corners down and breathed more easily. Then the cycle started over and the corners came alive again.

But something changed inside of me...a perspective shift.

I don't allow these items in my kitchen anymore.

They don't need to occupy that space, plus they wreak havoc with my sanity and my peace. And I need peace as much as I need just about anything else.

This is most likely a "way of life" for a long time, but I'm not going to act like I'm on "red alert" every day anymore. Like the BP meds I started taking when my first born was in kindergarten, pandemic supplies will have a place in my life, just not center stage.

I'm using the pandemic as an example but it is not the ONLY important issue for all of us.

Life is full of challenges to manage, adjust, and adapt. Curve balls happen every day. There are problems to solve, behaviors to change, and bridges to be built, for heaven's sake.

We find ways to live with all kinds of chaos, uncertainty, and daily protective behaviors. We do it when big life changes, good or bad come our way: job change, job loss, retirement, births, death, accidents, success, marriages, divorce, new homes, new relationships. We manage through all those big things and eventually move them into our own personal "normal".

In all of this adjustment, we move on, clearing the way for life!

This writing piece started out as one thing and became another thing, much like all the things in my head.

And as someone who sees the big things in life through the lens of the little things…it seems fitting to say that today and tomorrow I'll be clearing away a few more "countertops" in my life and I'll be doing that for quite some time.

Bit by bit, doing the small work to get to the big work of clearing the way for life…that's where I am right now.

Like the commercial for Capital One, I ask this question of you: What's on YOUR countertops?

There's Just Something About a Fire Pit

I stare into flames, watch them change shape, move the logs.

I watch the colors deepen, turning from red and orange, to white and blue hot, watch the purples play among the embers, feel the heat, the warmth, the peace, loving each flame.

I've come to the fire once again for renewal, reflection, for a communion of sorts.

I've come to be with God, to feel His presence. I've come knowing that the Spirit comes with me, leading me to where I need to be.

I'm here, at one of my favorite places…a huge and roaring fire pit. Not just any fire pit, this is the one at the home of my long time, good friend, Cathy Dybdahl.

Cathy and I were destined to be friends and neighbors. I like to think I had a quirky hand in her becoming my neighbor. It's a funny, weird little story of how God works in mysterious and sometimes humorous ways. And it is a story of how he takes the smallest of things and uses them for good. That story is for another time.

The important thing to know for now is that one of Cathy's main purposes on earth can be distilled into 3 words: "Loving others well." (Matthew 22:37-39) The fire pit plays a part in that.

This is no easy purpose to uphold. It takes a strong person to live out those words in a fierce and faithful manner. Fierce and faithful are also words that describe her and the fire she offers in her own backyard.

This particular fire pit has heard confessions of the heart from countless friends and family. It has been the scene of birthday parties, Thanksgiving and Christmas gatherings, "Bring your Adult kids to the fire" nights, Star Gazing by Fire Light, Friday night chill-out times, and even safe pandemic gatherings.

It has been my own personal retreat…my place to be quiet, listen, or to speak out, speak up, to bask in the light of friends' faces while the light and warmth of the fire pinks up our skin and makes everyone feel 10 years younger.

Often you will find a friend group, AKA, the Yayas, congregating around this friendly fire: Cathy, Judy, Colleen, Loreta, and me. I smile every time I think of these very distinctive, very wonderful women… rare, true friendship treasures.

No matter who is present around the circle, it is always a place of raucous laughter, deep and cleansing tears, hugs and holding close of those who need it the most on any given night. These women are all about support. We are single women and all but one has experienced the tragedy of divorce.

This life experience brings with it its own set of difficulties and pain that must be worked out and worked through in order to move on. Who best to do this with than others who have shared this same sorrow and victory?

Hearts are opened around the fire pit. People are kinder, gentler, quicker to reach out and connect with someone else's pathos and chaos.

People become good "neighbors" here, living out in real life what God asks of us for the eternal.

Plans are always in the works to pray and care for those whose names are mentioned at the fire. You can feel a part of a discipleship at this fire. Here… everyone matters. I belong here. And so does each soul sitting within reach of the fire's flames.

Each of us longs to belong!

Love & belonging constitute brick number 3 in the foundation of Maslow's Hierarchy of Needs, right after (2) safety & security and (1) food, water, shelter.

To actualize into the best we can be, we need all 5 of those foundational bricks.

To actualize spiritually we need holy fire.

The Holy Spirit calls us to transformative change, encourages and emboldens us to do and be the best that God intended us to be.

If you come to THIS fire to grow your faith, it is because the Holy Spirit has ignited that desire in you. A pathway from God to you exists. Your life's path is designed and colored specifically from your own individual personality, your own DNA.

Jesus is God with us. The Holy Spirit is God in us.

He knows us inside and out. He knows what moves us. It is one of His many ways to speak to us, guide us, prompt us, protect us, check and correct us, and at times hold a mirror to our faces for our own good. It's always for our own good, and the good of others. He is in the business of divine transformation!

He whispers to us in a breeze.
He moves us with his mighty wind.
He speaks to us in the flames.
He changes us by his fire.

He does everything in His power to reach us, speak to us, call us to action. He moves mountains in order to move our souls! This is love everlasting!

All we have to do is listen, open our hearts and minds to him, surrender to his good and perfect plan for us.

And, yes, sometimes we have to walk through fire here on earth.

There's no getting around that really.

It's hard, it's painful, sometimes it's even ugly.

When we walk through fire, we have two choices. We can succumb to destruction, or we can let the flames change us in ways we never would have learned otherwise.

Walking through fire can cleanse, refine and purify us… make us into the person God sees when He looks at our hearts!

The strength of overcoming makes us better people, more compassionate to others, stronger in many ways.

And if we really lean into the lesson, we can become mirrors to the world of how Christians are supposed to be here on earth. Not the tainted version of those who subversively use Christianity for their own cravings of power, who abuse the name of God in every self-serving action. No! Not those!

Instead, we can become the Christians whose main purpose is to love God and love our neighbors as ourselves, reflecting the glory of Christ in our actions and words. We then become true followers of Jesus and all that He is. That is the end game of the Holy Spirit's gift.

Holy Fire…powerful, personal, transformative.

Draw close to the fire!
Draw close to the One who knows how to create the best in you, how to transform every cell that makes up the unique in you and into the person He dreamed you to be.

What a wondrous thing to be at one with God.

He writes your story in the flames.
He offers a "new heart and a new spirit".
That's the wonder of God, the Three in One.

Ezekial 36:26- *"I will give you a new heart and put a new spirit in you; I will remove from you your heart of stone and give you a heart of flesh."*

2 Corinthians 3:18- *"We can all draw close to him with the veil removed from our faces. And with no veil, we all become like mirrors who brightly reflect the glory of the Lord Jesus. We are being transfigured into his very image as we move from one brighter level of glory to another. And this glorious transfiguration comes from the Lord, who is the Holy Spirit."*

(Dedicated to the Yayas)

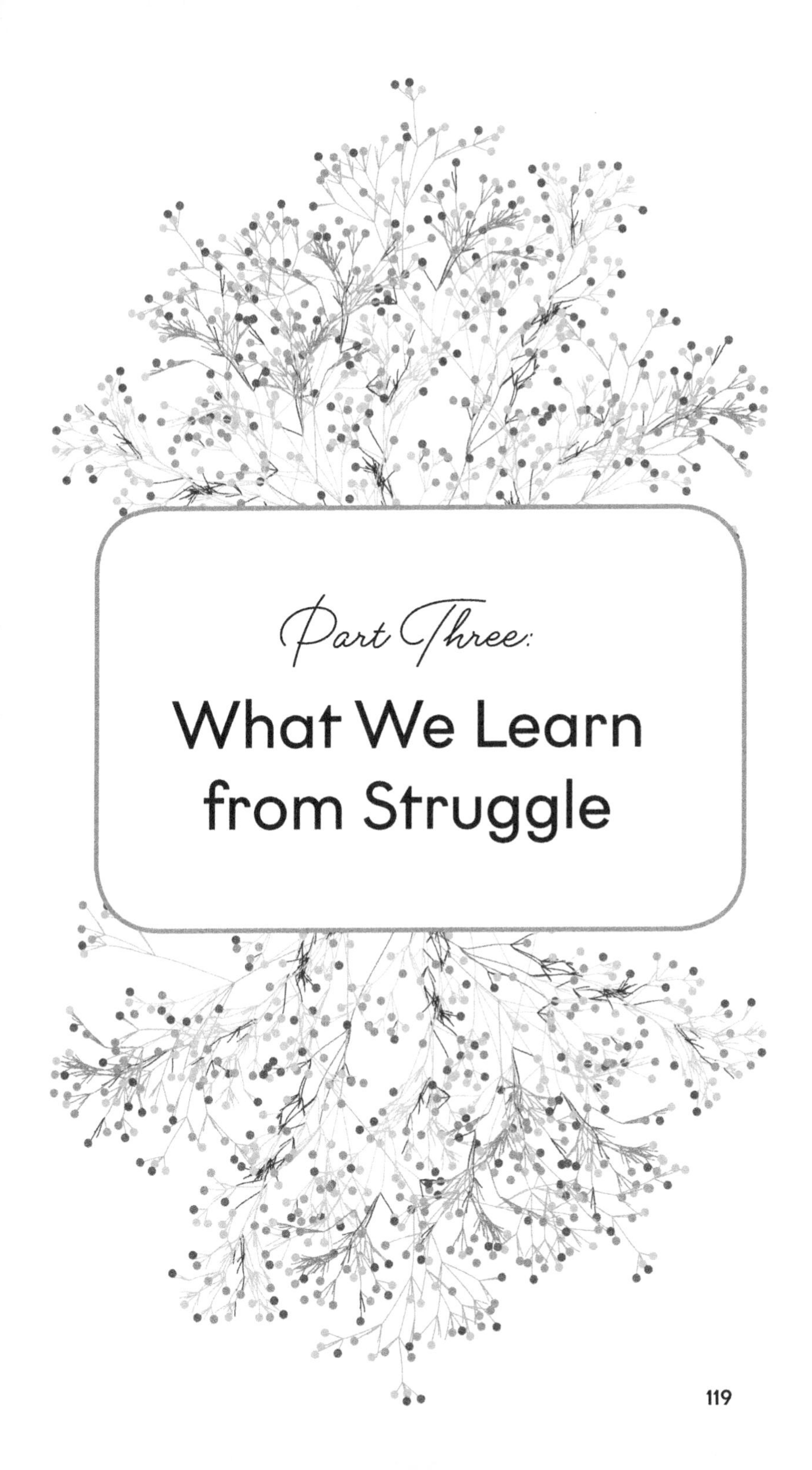

Part Three:

What We Learn from Struggle

Out of the Overflow

Romans 7:15 "For I do not understand my own actions. I do not do what I want, but I do the very thing I hate."

Matthew 12:34 "For out of the overflow of the heart the mouth speaks."

Each day I struggle. I'm a study in contradiction.
What I want to do, I do not do.
What I want to say, I do not say.

And every time this happens, I say I'll do better next time.

How can we want to say or do the right thing so much, and yet the wrong words come out of our mouths or pour out onto texts and emails with disappointing regularity.

Every day, we are bombarded with negative thinking, combative words, unthinkable photos. How much can we take before we run and bury our heads in our iPhones or hide behind the soothing monotony of TV and Instagram reels.

Sometimes we run to our pantries or our homemade bars to dull our stress.

We even spew negativity ourselves and become sickened by the echo of our own words

How do we break away from doing exactly what we do not intend to do?

Luke says it all starts with the heart. I think he's right.

To change our words and behaviors, we could start by examining what we put into our minds, and what we feed our souls.

Maybe we take a look at how we act day in and day out.

How good are we at exhibiting self-control in difficult situations?

We are given opportunity after opportunity to practice holding our tongues.

Are we a little too eager to honk our horns, or tail gate the slow driver?

Are we a little too impatient with the person in front of us who has 20 items for the 12-item fast checkout lane?

Do we see someone drop a piece of paper or heaven forbid, their mask and immediately assume they're irresponsible?

Do we hear a mother at the playground speak frustratingly to her 6-year-old and instantly believe she is a "bad mom"?

Do we see someone rush ahead of us and assume they are an entitled person?

Do we see a photo and rush to judgment about it?

Do we hide behind that old and lazy excuse, "That's just who I am"?

If you mentally checked "yes" to any of these, join me in the oh-so-human race.

I don't know exactly what we are racing to, but we're doing it at break neck speeds.

So maybe slowing down is part of the answer, or at least pausing to think before we spew.

If we hit the "pause" button on quick judgments and negative perceptions, what might we get in their place?

Would it be Patience? Forgiveness? Kindness? Love?

I think these would be a welcome addition to our thoughts and actions and go a long way toward becoming the humans we really want to be. Who wouldn't want an overflow of love?

Travel Notes: Each One Matters

I wrote Travel Notes for those who sometimes feel a little out of place; for those who go it alone, or have lost trust in themselves or for those who are just plain tired. I am a realistic optimist, so I see life as a big, beautiful mess, full of wonder. But I also understand the pain and discomfort that can accompany that beautiful mess.

Travel Notes are for those who may feel unseen, unheard, less than, or misunderstood. I recognize that when we feel that way, even if it is temporary, our world becomes harder; time with others feels off; thoughts and emotions become tangled and misconstrued.

Maybe reading one of these notes will fit your situation and ease you back on track, or at least remind you that you matter!

For Those Who are Tired:

You don't have to prove yourself.

You don't have to do more to count.

You don't have to say "yes" to every ask.

You have the right and sometimes the need to say "no".

It's okay to rest, take a break from your endless lists.

You can stop... Or you can put the world on pause if that's what you need.

The world will spin on and spin out, even when you are not standing.

Let someone else stand in your place for just a bit.

Rest and rejoin ... refreshed.

For those who are on the right side of defiance:

Do you know just how strong you are?

I may know your story…or at least I know some of that story.
And you are one courageous warrior.

You are a force to be reckoned with.

I know you do not feel that you are right now.
You may be your own harshest critic.

That seems to be our nature in times like these.

Change the tape for one minute.
Rewind and start uncovering the truth.

The truth is you have already stood up to your adversary.
You have already said the words & done what is right.

You just haven't given yourself credit for those hard-won victories.

You've been pinned in the corner.
You've been dissed out loud.
You've been underestimated.
Underplayed.
Overstepped.
You've been hit while you've been down.
Below the belt and above all reason.

But I don't see anyone standing over you, counting you OUT now!
Not one.
They wouldn't dare.
The thing is you took the blows, went into your corner and decided you would not surrender to something that was dead wrong, so wrong, it could not even stand for one minute in the presence of truth without flinching.
You stared the bully in the face and said, NO!
Not for me!
I know what is right for me, for those I love, for the future and my future self.
And it is not this.

You brought up your armor of Truth and held firm.

You held on to Goodness, Kindness, Faith.

You made your actions match your words; your thoughts mirror your heart.

And you stood and said I will not take the easy way out, even if it brings me pain yet again. Even if it causes me to lose what I had worked so hard to regain.

Even with all of that, I will not bend to the easy way out.

I will not give up what is true, right, pure, unselfish, or what is love!

For what IS love if it has none of these other things?

Response to adversary:

Save your lengthy sentences and your jumbled logic; your long lines of self-justification.

They are nothing to me.
They mean nothing to me now.

I will focus on what is best and what is good and that will be my guide.

For I am on the right side of defiance, and you are not in charge of my life or my soul.

I am.

For Those Who Hide Behind Smiles:

You are not as invisible as you think.

I have looked into your eyes that are trying so hard to match the emotion you want to send to the world ...the one you think the world needs you to send, and my heart leaps out to you.

I know that smile. I understand. I have walked that path; smiled that smile.

I see the person and the need behind the smile.

I see your many bruises and scars.

I see your hesitancy, your anger, your understandable distrust.

I see your unquestionable worth and strength.

You may not know this, but there are those who stand beside you even when you remain silent. They notice you.

They want to shout that you aren't obligated to hide your true emotions.

But that choice is yours.

Do what you need to feel safe. Go ahead and smile even when you are hurting, IF it keeps you safe, or if that's what moves you forward or simply moves you past.

There are those who ***will*** see you and ***will be there*** if you need a place to be truly and lovingly seen. And in that place no pretend smiles are needed.

For Those Who Stand alone in life:

You don't have to do it all...

Even though all of it is on your plate.

You don't have to pretend you are ok when you are not.

You don't have to make excuses.

You don't have to explain yourself to anyone.

There are those who want to stand with you, to walk alongside you, to help and be helped by you.

When you feel safe, let them in.

For Those Who Feel Unloved & Unloving in this moment:

Whatever you do, don't let the world's definition of "love" trip you up.

Instead, think about how love shows up in your life...and embrace it
Don't let those who may not have your best interests at heart define your worth.

You deserve the best life has to offer.

Patience is your friend and your teacher. So is persistence.

Stay in the game. Trust those who stay in the game with you.

And take comfort in this: Those who fall away...out of your life...were supposed to fall away.

Trust that others more worthy of your time and your love are out there ready to be recognized, ready for the door to be opened by you.

God specializes in surprises! Many gifts await you. So, keep your eyes open for the unexpected.

He knows your heart's desire. And He wants you to have it.

Matthew 6:21 "Delight yourself in the Lord, and He will give you the desires of your heart."

For The Parents Among Us

First things first...you are the very definition of brave.

No matter your circumstances, every day you move forward to do the next thing that needs to be done.

Shrug off outsider voices who have no stake in the lives of your family.
Listen only to those you trust...those who have invested in your well-being and those of your children.

And listen to yourself...especially yourself.
Trust your own instincts.

Write the golden moments down somewhere. You will be glad you did, 10, 20, 50 years from now.

Write the hard knock moments down too.

You will come back to those and see how much victory you had over them. You will be able to give yourself some credit for all your hard-won moments as a parent.

Build a village of trusted adults who can help or give insight all the way to graduation and beyond.

No kidding...you need the village that long. Parenting adult children is not as easy as it may sound. It takes a while to

find your footing in this phase of life. The key here is to give advice only when asked.
Give your child the generational gift of unconditional love!
That is the best gift you can give.
Everything you are doing, you are doing for love...pure, stand-up love!

God has knit the soul of your child in a beautiful way...ready to receive the unique gifts you have to offer.

Trust in God and the village you have built.

Although it may feel like it for a while, you are not alone.

For Those Who Have Lost Trust in Someone:

When you lose trust in someone, there is a feeling of constant guardedness and pain that follow you around for decades.

Initially it's a kick in the gut; a sudden loss of balance; and a shocking realization that everything is out of order.

And here's the real kicker: It takes many steps to build trust but only one to tear it down.
And once it is gone, it is hard to regain.
It not only affects your present relationship, but also everyone in the future to some degree.

Trust is a hard-won building block in the foundation of relationships.

It is tested in a million little moments, not just the main events.

Trust can be rebuilt. It will just take time and the tests of consistency.
That person will have to show up in every avenue that was destroyed.

The person willing to take the time to rebuild trust in *all* the ways it needs rebuilding is at least a contender for your love or your friendship.

It's a good first step. And eventually you will know if it is good enough. Trust yourself to know.

The Linda Beth "Sparkle!"

Top: Linda Huling
Bottom: Jared, Kathryn, Josh

Top: Brenda Jo Elder "When We Were Young and Glorious"
Bottom: Linda Floyd Huling, Jerry Watson, Lettie (The Floyd Sisters)

Top: "Sweet Flower Revival"
Bottom: "Little Buddy"

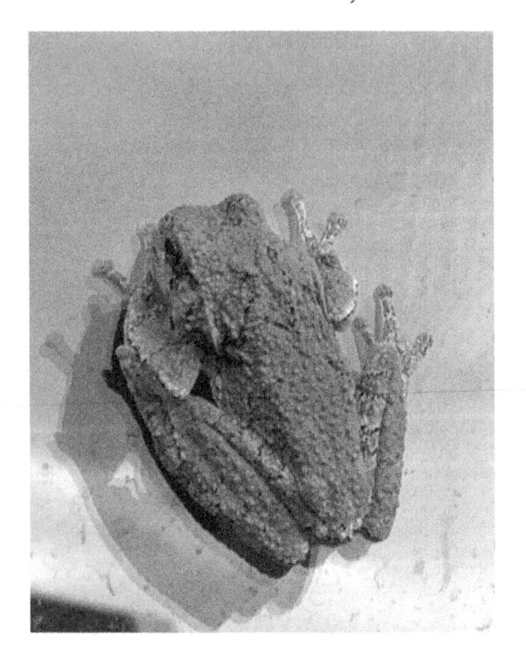

Top: Autumn on my deck
Bottom: The goddesses: Top Row-Nancy, Jeanne, Lori, Linda W.
Bottom Row-Helen, Linda H., Mary

Top: Linda W., Lori, Sandy
Bottom: The goddesses: Sandy, Mary, Lori, Jeanne, Helen, Linda H. "A Safe Place"

Top: THE Fire Pit from "There's Something about a Fire Pit"
Bottom: "There's Something about a Fire Pit"

Top: Cathy Dybdahl
Bottom: The Yayas: Top Row-Colleen Hamons, Linda Huling
Bottom Row-Cathy Dybdahl, Loreta, Judy Cook

Top: The Yayas: Colleen Hamons, Cathy Dybdahl, Judy Cook, Loreta
Bottom: Hope rock - "Rock of Ages"

Top: Hope Daisy - "Rock of Ages"
Bottom: Kathryn, as Belle - "Out of the Mouths of Babes"

Christ Church, United Methodist- "Hope is the Thing"

Sister and brother-in-law: Jerry and Jim Watson

Top: Sister, Jerry
Bottom: Sister, Lettie

Top: Brother-in-law, Ed and sister Lettie
Bottom: Ed

Top: Kathryn, Chester R. Floyd, Geraldine Floyd, Jared
Bottom: Mother, Geraldine Davis Floyd

Top: Father, Chester R. Floyd
Bottom: Jared, (son)

Top: Kathryn, Jared, Josh
Bottom: Jared (son)

Top: Josh and Kathryn Moore (son-in-law and daughter)
Bottom: Kathryn and Josh Moore

Top: Kathryn Moore (daughter)
Bottom: Linda and Kathryn

Top: Betsy (cousin)
Bottom: Linda, Hal and Ann Mathews, Karen and Peter Huling

Top: Pepper Moore (best grand dog)
Bottom: Yankee Huling (beloved pet 2000-2013)

Top: Linda
Bottom: Terrie

Top: Debbie Nofziger
Bottom: Elaine

Top: Phyllis Pilewski
Bottom: Mari Hall

If you cannot reconcile who someone is now with what you believe matters most in life, that is a clear warning signal to set your heart on "pause", take a breath, and keep your eyes wide open.

Watch out for a lack of empathy. That's a big flag, painted bright red.
A lack of clear communication, even more so a disinterest in communicating is a telltale red flag as well.

Look for consistent behaviors. I don't remember where I read this first, but it has become one of my litmus tests: "People eventually tell you who they are. Listen to what they are saying."

Search for the things that will tell you where that person's heart is; what their priorities are; and how they communicate when life gets hard.
How you work through hurdles together is a predictor of what the next 50 years together will look like.

Trust does not contain a "one size fits all" list of parameters. You get to decide.

Don't let being betrayed in the past rob you of today's joy or tomorrow's relationship.

Some day you will trust again.
And you want to be healthy enough to recognize and enjoy that relationship when it comes your way.

Enough!

I lift my voice to my creator,
The One who made and understands me.

The One who knows the intentions of my heart and the motivations behind my actions.
The One who knows the Truth.

He knows every stick and every stone that makes its mark,
Then rights the wrong from His merciful heart.

He takes the harsh condemning tapes and stops the 'spin' at once.
"Enough", commands the Lord.

He quiets the din in my beleaguered mind like the brilliant conductor that He is.

And He points me gently back to His Voice, the only voice I need.
And I remember whose I am.

"Enough", soothes the Lord, "You are enough."
His words pierce my soul. His mercy is pure!
The well of His understanding runs deep into my being.

And I am filled with peace, with blessed assurance that He is mine.
More than enough…His love is more than enough for me.

Despair and disappointment ebb and exit out of my lungs.
I breathe in the calm that only He can bring.
And I know without a doubt that hope has come and I am enough because I am His.

Grief Comes in Bits and Pieces

Grief comes in bits and pieces!

It blasts through the screen like a crazed, jilted lover, ready to exact its due.

It overwhelms and robs you of the very breath you are struggling to control.

It grabs hold of our insides and wrings us dry.

Grief is the fibromyalgia of feelings!

It sneaks in when you least expect it; slithers under your door and enters your day in every bone, muscle, thought and feeling.

Grief is the uninvited visitor.

It comes unbidden in the middle of the night, waking you with sorrow that sucker punches your solar plexus with way too much power for your 3:00 AM soul to manage.

It comes unwanted in the middle of the day, shoving its way into a lively conversation at lunch.

It startles you while you're working, robbing you of the peace of distracted 'busyness'.

It shatters holidays with one look at photos of your loved one's face, and the first note of once joyful songs you sang together.

It is "too much with us".

Grief, the relentless, unmerciful teacher, demands that we let it run its course.

For in the end, the expression of grief, as horrible and as punishing as it can be, is the main 'way through'…a bridge to the other side of sorrow.

We grieve deeply because we love deeply.

And one day in a moment of grief, our pain is at last bearable.

Tears of sorrow become tears of healing.

Painful memories turn into reminders of a cherished love.

Tender souls in the midst of sorrow.

Grief comes in bits and pieces over time, for the rest of our lives.

For if we guard our hearts from life's pain and loss, we'll never truly live or feel the depth of love.

Grief comes because love came before.

Bring on wretched grief...and bring it to the full... it's the price we paid because we felt at all.

The Relentless Circle of Life

My grandfather was a coal miner and a hunter. He used his gun to put food on the table for two families. He was also the kindest, gentlest man, who played with children at his feet after 12 hours in a dangerous underground cave. He was a good man and I loved him deeply.

Nature calls for a "circle of life" because what is predator today, may be prey tomorrow.

Talking on my friend's porch one morning, ready to leave, I noticed yellow finches flying in and out of her shrubs. She said it was their daily gathering site. I smiled. The thought of birds congregating made me happy.

Moments later I was nearing my car and saw a hawk flying low, then rising with the tiniest bit of yellow in its talons. The sly predator had taken advantage of the moment when my friend and I had walked away from the gathering site and jetted in to find its vulnerable prey.

I stood at my car immobilized as I watched the hawk power through the space between me and its landing spot. I felt sick to my stomach. I heard myself whimper. And I couldn't help it, I started to cry.

I will never be able to witness the vulnerable being overpowered by the strong and the wily without having my heart broken.

Never.

It is the stuff of my nightmares.

I know it happens. I understand it is survival.

But I feel powerless to help. And I detest that feeling.

I think of the world and how it has always been broken into uneven groups of the vulnerable and the powerful.

And I think of my place in it.

Being sick to my stomach is not enough. Tears are not enough.

All around there are opportunities to intervene, to reach out, to rescue.

To help the helpless.

What can I do right now that will matter?

How can I hold my own actions accountable?

I want to judge less, fear less, and act more on behalf of those who cannot.

Let me never stand by inanely immobile.

Let me never harden my heart to the needs of others.

Use all of me for all of those.

Brown Light

Her world is brown.
Brown bits caked in a bowl, cracked with time.
Faded brown walls, closing in.
Dirty blonde hair, straggling across a flat pillow.
Dark, brown blood on dingy sheets,
Mixed with nameless stains, aged and long forgotten.

Muted sounds through too thin walls,
Lines on the ceiling form familiar patterns…imaginary faces, shapes
Tell a story when no books can.

Dusty cells cascading downward, land on her face and hair…
Helpless to stop the endless cycle of life…from dust to dust.

Her world is faded brown, in a wordless bowl,
Where time trudges when it cannot march.

The door opens.
The faintest breeze catches the overhead fan, moving the air in a slow and steady beat.
From the door, a startled, hesitant beginning.
From the bed, a blurred view.
And…
Color enters her world in a dizzying whirl of blue, green and white, now moving quickly toward her.
Pale skin, deep, brown eyes, fierce and full of purpose.
…and something else.

They're all she can see now.
Brown eyes, burning with light and tears, urge her up.
Color and Light enter her soul,
…and something else …an unfamiliar feeling …strength.
She takes a full and deep breath of air.

She forces dulled senses back to life.

Sounds form into words.

"Come! I'll help you. We're leaving."

Words of hope and light…brown light.

He is her son, her savior. He is her light.

Just a Little More Time

All I want is just a little more time to watch you closely, look at your face, oh so carefully.

To watch your smile move from your eyes to your wrinkled lips in record time.

Or notice your eyebrows raise in that playful way as I talk on and on about my day.

A little more time to rest in the warmth of your love.

A little more time on the porch swinging and singing, with your arm around my back and my head on your shoulder.

More time in the back yard enjoying the fruits of your labor, pulling tomatoes from their vines or picking cherries for pies; grapes for jam. Or just to watch you prop your foot on the sturdy weathered stump and take a look around at your place of peace… slowing the pace of time.

Just a little more time to linger on the old, metal glider and talk about life, love, and loss; to mull over today's questions and tomorrow's plans.

More time to walk briskly with you in the park; then slow our pace as you spot mayapples, masquerading as mini-umbrellas under a tree or point to the tiny bluets that tempt us toward summer.

To find the place where wishes were made on wispy dandelions and hopeful smiles were shared along our favorite path. More time to gather the wisdom you had stored in decades of living.

More time to knead the dough, or roll out the crust, while puffs of flour and laughter were caught in the rays of sunshine from the kitchen window.

More time to feel the gentle breezes flowing from your open transom and believe that all is right with the world again.

A little more time to bask in your sacred love, to be the star in your world, and the light in your eyes.

Just a little more time to appreciate the depth of your understanding, to hold on to your strength and feel complete acceptance.

I need more time to gather all your hope, your insight, your kindness and all of YOU that will fill me full of bright promises and hope for tomorrow.

I want more time with you…just a little more. Time to ask the questions I never asked!

To tell you how much I loved every single part of you!

I see you everywhere…across the street, walking in that purposeful way of yours, in the art museum, in the checkout line at the grocery. I try to catch up but it's never really you.

I think I hear your voice as I doze off in my chair. I startle awake and listen with every cell I have. But the only sound I hear is the murmur of my own disappointed heart.

Years later in my dreams I finally see you clearly...looking calm, untroubled... so whole.

I watch, mesmerized as you glide toward me, smiling so confidently.

I see you bend to relax on a bench in a garden.

I watch as you tilt your head, pat the seat next to you, and smile at me once more.

Somehow, I know you are telling me all is well for you, and all will be well for me until one day I sit beside you on that bench and hold your hand for all eternity.

That's all I want.

The Downside of Perfection

Pacing on my deck, puzzling through an unresolved issue, I lifted my head to release the tension in my neck. My attention was stolen by creamy clouds all billowy and blue in the western sky. But the formations were "off". Cotton-ball cumulus clouds were directly in my sightline, but off to the side were gray stratus blankets holding on to that section of sky. They don't normally team up that close in pleasant weather. They weren't what I was expecting because they weren't the picture-perfect paintings you see in coffee-table books.

This messy hop-scotch version was more compelling than a perfect one.

And of course, I think about what this means in my life and the days of wanting everything to be picture-perfect. I wonder what I've missed by holding on to that impossible standard.

Consider these little slices of life:

- You've had a lovely morning with your 2-year-old and now you're at the grocery with that same, now hungry 2-year-old, in need of a nap or some cheerios. Her tired cries echo in the aisles. And while you scramble to grab the last item and rush to the check out, you hear yourself making apologies for your child. Your beautiful, hungry child!
- You find yourself during picture-taking time, shuffling to the back, trying to find the right way to pose. Wondering if you're wearing black yet again? Or wondering if you are showing enough teeth in this smile, and wishing you had brushed your hair.

Kind of takes away from the moment, doesn't it?

I don't think having our "best life" has anything to do with having a perfect life. There's really no such thing! Perfection is just a mere illusion accompanied by a heavy hammer of expectation.

Show me your messy house and I'll find the love tucked in all those tousled corners.

Show me games and bags of banana gram tiles stacked on shelves, flour spilled on your countertops next to 5 kinds of tea, and I'll know I've landed in the coziest place on the block.

Show me your yard with weeds and I'll happily understand that the clover and persistent dandelions are nourishing the bees, and all is right with the world.

Give me a selfie where everyone's hair is a frightful mess, where the shamelessly, open-mouthed smiles tell you they are having the time of their lives.

Give me real friends, honest conversations, the raw and the real.

Tell me what you are actually thinking. I don't need your thoughts to be all shined up before you share them with me.

I want to know what you are feeling, even when those feelings are prickly, sad, jumbled... especially then.

And when it's my turn to be the farthest thing from perfect, or tumble off that pedestal I had no need to be on in the first place, and I go over the edge with disappointment in myself, I need you to say:

"Hey! It's ok that you don't have it right yet. You'll figure it out."

Or...

"That mistake was in the past. Let it go!"

"Nobody's perfect."

I've come to realize that:

- When we live closest to our own genuine selves, is when we shine the best.
- Gap-toothed grins make everybody smile.
- Unexpected cloud formations remind us of our own imperfect beauty.

Now, isn't that just perfect!

I Don't Have to Choose!

It isn't "either-or" with you

I don't have to choose

You love me too
Not after this ...or after that...
You love me when, you love me where

You heal me too
Not at the end of the list
You put me first…how can that be?

The prayers of others carry me…

Through the roof and to the floor at your feet
At your feet, I look into the Eyes of Mercy
The Face of Grace

I don't have to choose
I don't have to sacrifice my needs

You did that too

You sacrificed for me long ago
You bled and died and rose again, just for me and all mankind
You did this once
So that through all time we are loved and we are saved

Your love is big
Bigger than I, bigger than my request

I can ask
Ask big
And I can ask again

You will hear me
Heal me
Love me

And Your love will heal me

My needs placed in the Hand of Mercy

I ask and I receive
I doubt and then believe
I stumble and am given ground on which to stand
I fail and am caught by the love that holds me up
I crumble and am given faith to move forward

I fall and you whisper, “Rise up and walk”

Your YES is bigger than my doubts
Your WAIT is wiser than my plan
Your NO smooths my edges, sharpens my reach

Your love makes me stronge
I call out and you answer.

I don’t have to choose!

The Inside Out

I cry out overwhelmed from sadness that can't be soothed.

Helpless to find anything good.

I can't concentrate…can't make the airline reservation without thinking why I need to go, or without step-by-step help. I can't even recall how my name is written on my license so I can fill in the flight information.

Where are the many pens I own? Where is the paper?

I'm writing on a napkin and it's falling apart from my tears.

I can't catch my breath…The word "cancer" has overcome my senses.

How can that word be associated with my child? My child and not me!

I continue down to the level of crazy…then I catch myself…and don't know what to do with all this out-of-control emotion.

Where does it go except straight to my heart. Anxiety hits hard. The useless mantra "be strong" just makes me weak.

How can I calm my heart from its jumps and jostles in my chest…ready to attack the rest of itself and implode.

Inside me a battle is being fought and I have no shield.

Swollen vessels have turned against me.

I feel like I'm self-destructing from the inside out.

I'm weeping from the inside out.

God, I know you hear me.

I know you will steady me… I just need to breathe and to wait.

But the interminable waiting strains my chest.

Steady one minute, doubting the next.

You alone know every detail and what is ahead.

That is enough for now…for this minute.

I think of the childhood song…"…little ones to Him belong, they are weak, and He is strong."

His voice whispers, "Lean on me now".

I feel strength begin to spread throughout my body.

Untangled, I can breathe again.

"For when I am weak, then I am strong." 2 Corinthians 12:10

Sound Beat

Hear the beating of the drums that drown out dreams.

Senseless striving to overtake and overwhelm.

What is the point of endless acts
of punching clocks and counting tasks.

The pressured beat sprints on, then soundly self-destructs.

Slow the pace!

Slow the frantic race… or hearts will give out, as minds wear out.

And earnest souls will sell out.

Till the shadow of our impact finally fades out.

Hear the urgent beating of the drums
that speak from within and not without.

Words

She had to say something. She couldn't stand it any longer.

"It's been 100 days! Can you imagine?"

He looked up from his papers, confused and annoyed, "What are you talking about?"

"The hostages. They've been in captivity for a hundred days now. And there's no sign of change." Her breath was shaky, "Can you imagine what their fear must be like? I keep thinking about their families."

"I don't know anything about it. I've been working 12-hour days." Ethan focused back on his work, "I don't have time for this."

"Here's what..." she started to catch him up on the news.

"Look, Grace," he cut in, "I have a brief to finish by the time we land, so could you stop talking, stop asking me questions? This case is everything. It's life or death to my career."

"Of course," her voice smaller now. "Sure, Ethan".

Life or death.

There was nothing to see on this road. The moonless night hid anything of interest and the putrid heat made her feel like she was inhaling stale water. The only lights were from oncoming cars and the monotony was making her edgy...or was it the silence.

The silence, like this drive to the Everglades, was lasting an eternity.

"How is it that we never make time to talk, even when we are captives in a car."

The question she had asked lingered in the air like an unwelcome stench.

Ethan's fingers on the wheel tapped out impatience, irritation, aggravation, but no response.

The sound from the road was chiding rhythmically, "Empty, empty. No words. No words."

Where were her own words? She needed to find the right ones soon.

The ridiculously expensive diamond on her finger felt too tight, burned too bright. Was she expecting too much?

And the words died on the edge of her tongue.

The Everglades behind them, estimates piled up for the home they were building together. Decisions on lots and plots were left unmade. Finding compromise was a joke as there was never time to talk it through.

On yet another exhausted evening, they committed to dinner at 6:00 to finalize at least the first decision. She ordered tea and checked her mail. At 6:30, she ordered an appetizer and wine to make it worth the waiter's time.

A chime on her phone delivered his message, "Something came up, be there soon".

At 8:00 she asked for the check and laid down the money and a generous tip.

He entered the room, and his eyes found hers. The veil came off and she saw not love, only his resignation and impatience. What she felt was relief.

She fingered the familiar ring, edged it off and laid it down beside the check.

No words needed.

Life or death. Sometimes you get to choose.

Part Four:

What We Learned from a World-Wide Pandemic

Chronicling the Pandemic in 2020

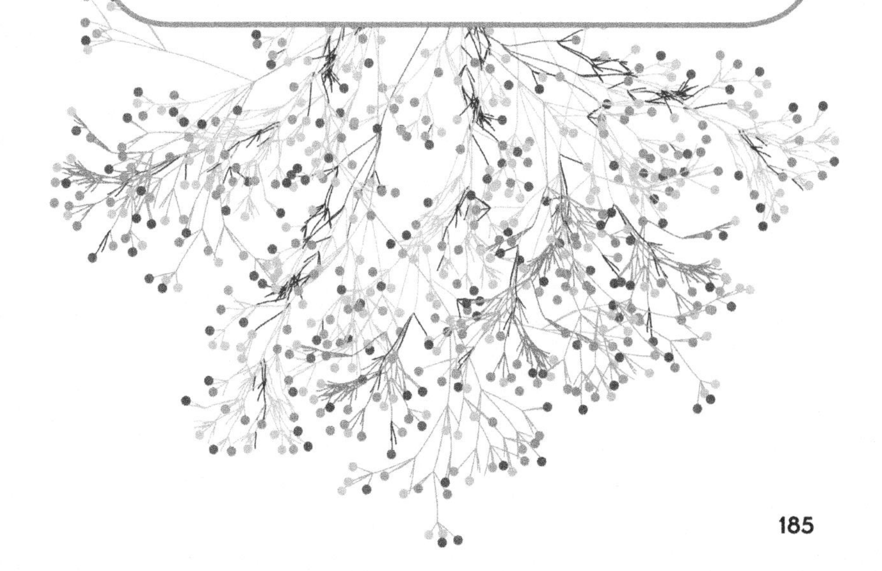

And the Heroes Rise Up

written March 28, 2020,

amended in 2022

There's no getting around it.

Life, as we knew it, changed somewhere around early January, 2020.

Most of us didn't know it at the time, but change with a capital C for Coronavirus, entered our lives, hiding in plain sight and lying in wait for us to notice. And it was multiplying in an insidiously treacherous way.

Some had seen the writing on the wall before the rest of us.

The scientists knew. The researchers knew. The epidemiologists knew.

Many were vocal about its coming, long before January 2020.

One in particular the brilliant Anthony Fauci, MD, NIAID Director (National Institute of Allergy and Infectious Diseases), had dedicated his life's work to just this type of virus warfare and had been sounding the gong for a long time. His worst nightmare, the thing that kept him awake at night, had arrived and was landing on our door knobs and grocery carts from sea to shining sea.

79-year-old Dr. Fauci, became the truth teller for our country… the man with the scientific plan.

He was the voice who set the record straight with the confidence of someone who has long ago eschewed exaggerations and any trace of ego. He was the doctor we relied on to tell us what was happening and what to do next, all based on scientific evidence.

He was an interesting mix of straight shooter and diplomat. He found a way to save face for those who got carried away. He linked hope with science and he made sense. He saved lives.

After more than 50 years in government, Fauci stepped down from his position of NIAID Director in December of 2022. The next generation of biomedical research will take the lead. Dr. Fauci's story is not over yet. The world will continue to benefit from his wisdom and his expertise. Thank you, good doctor!

Pandemic Palms

Written on April 5, 2020

For once in our lives, we can say that we have something in common with every person on earth! We are all going through this pandemic together, like it or not.

I have experienced 69 Palm Sundays in my life so far, and not one of them ever looked like this one.

Tomorrow I will be having virtual Communion with my church. And even the bread I baked for the occasion is not enough to offset this odd way to worship on Palm Sunday, the start of Holy Week.

Notice I did not capitalize the word "pandemic" earlier. I don't want to give it any more power than it should have in my life. It already has way too much.

But Holy Week, I'll capitalize that! I need to get some things in perspective, and place power where power should be.

In John 12:12-13 we are told, "The next day the great crowd that had come for the Feast heard that Jesus was on his way to Jerusalem. They took palm branches and went out to meet him, shouting, "Hosanna! Blessed is he who comes in the name of the Lord! Blessed is the King of Israel!"

The palm branches strewn over the pathway for Jesus represented the path of victory and triumph. They also meant goodness and peace.

Those in Jerusalem felt that Jesus was coming to be their political king, to save them from the Romans. But you know how that story goes. Jesus never does the expected thing. He had a different plan. He wasn't there to rule the Romans. He was there because He rules the world.

First and foremost, He was the world's savior. He is the King of Kings!

And Jesus was playing the "long game" for mankind.

We, however, want the short game…the quick fix…always have.

We want this pandemic OVER and DONE …wrapped up yesterday.

That's how I have felt many times about Covid-19. I want it to be over. I want to play my part, whatever that entails, and within a few weeks, a couple of months at the most, I want it gone.

I want that victory stroll into Jerusalem, palms at our feet, and I want to be gathered together for the feast with the ones I love. But that is not how pandemics go. And this one is playing a pernicious game of hide and seek as it also plays its own long game.

I don't know about you, but my prayer list has grown so long that I moved it to a spiral notebook.

I approach that prayer list as if I am doing battle…I am praying my way through this pandemic in more ways than one. And when I remember that is my focus, I do a whole lot better.

The list reminds me of a shorter one I used in 2011 & 2013 when each of my knees took turns being replaced with titanium.

In the home recovery part where I was working to get a perfect straight leg and a perfect bending knee, there was an exercise my physical therapist offered.

It was a killer exercise where you lie on your stomach, leg extended well over the edge of a surface with a 5-pound weight holding it down. This torture is necessary for the straightening process to be fine-tuned.

The leg must be held straight out. And it is held for 5 minutes each time, several times a day.

I am a strong, tough old bird, but this exercise always brought tears to my eyes…and each time that 5 minutes had the potential to feel like 5 days.

To take my focus off of the pain and onto a better place, I laid a short prayer list in front of my eyes, impossible issues that I brought before God.

Prayers for friends, family, and one whopper for myself. I figured the most difficult requests would force me to concentrate all my mind, body and soul on those and nothing else.

During that time of sacred torture, I prayed some of my most fervent prayers. With my leg suspended in torture, I offered it all to God, in 5-minute intervals of mind over matter.

My habit was to set the timer. I was always surprised when it was over. Most of the time I was still finishing the prayers as I lowered my body away from the pain.

Relief and peace would flow through my body.

God took a painfilled 5 minutes and turned it into an altar of powerful prayer.

That's how I need to refocus on this pandemic Palm Sunday.

There is much to do, and our worst days are yet to be experienced, but we can't let up.

We must balance the weight of it all on our bodies and minds, knowing that if we persevere, we can straighten this out.

We know there will be no shortcut and no easy path. We just have to keep doing the next right thing…for the good of all mankind, at this pivotal time in our lives.

A very wise Paul said, "We must not get tired of doing good, for we will reap a harvest at the proper time if we don't give up." Galatians 6:9

May the branches of Peace and Goodness be yours this Palm Sunday!

The Heroes Among Us

written April 12, 2020

Hope is a curious thing. It can be the thing that eludes us, or the thing that guides us.

A 'once in a lifetime' horror entered our stratosphere and was met with acts of 'once in a lifetime' heroism. A deadly pandemic vs. a determined world.

I pray this will not become a "man vs man" war.

Bringing something good out of something bad is the very definition of transformative hope.

And isn't hope the "stuff that heroes are made of"?

So far, the coronavirus pandemic has been a calculatingly cruel teacher. It has run us ragged cramming for the final exam. What we know to be true changes daily as we race toward an indecipherable finish line. And that finish line is still such an unknown that it is drawn oh, so lightly with a pencil.

We need hope.

And we need heroes like we need solid ground to walk on again.

One thing this experience has taught me is that acts of bravery know no age or job title. Bravery is the equalizer of our times right now!

And while the virus knows no borders, neither do the heroes among us.

They are rising up in not just the obvious corners, but also in the quieter places of our lives.

There are so many I am going to put them in three functional categories.

Here are some of their descriptions.

(1) The Frontliners

Meanwhile, all over America, and all over our entire globe, the Frontliners are doing the hard, critical things.

-- Among the many sacrificial workers are the doctors, nurses, medical technicians, nursing home employees, pharmacists, fire fighters, EMTS, paramedics, police forces, the national guard.

Some are recognizable in their white coats, or green hospital garb, their bright red or blue uniforms, their stethoscopes around their necks and their long lanyards full of official badges...badges of honor!

What they see and face day and night is truly sacrificial service.

Their stories will always be unimaginably selfless, some even miraculous.

Their purpose is clear. They are risking their lives every day so that others can live!

We owe them a debt we can never repay, and one we should never forget.

I am humbled by their courage, awed by their proficiency, and brought to tears by their overwhelming selflessness. May God keep them safe.

--Not all Frontliners wear uniforms. They are heroes in plain clothes and in plain sight.

The supply chain heroes and the critical jobs of 'everyday life' are about as essential as it gets.

From company owners to every single worker and industry we owe our grateful thanks. This list is also lengthy: groceries, the construction industry, the restaurant industry, transportation companies, refuse companies, the United States Mail workers, electricians, plumbers and so many more create, provide and transport our every single need.

We could not function without them! "Neither snow, nor rain, nor pandemic viruses" will get in the way of their production and delivery. They risk their lives as well because they are our "on the move" heroes, operating where the virus multiplies.

They work with smiles on their faces, patience in their behaviors, and a dedication that is unbelievable. I am blown away by every mail deliverer who, in spite of the lack of protective gloves and masks, still goes to work every day without fail.

(2) The Hidden Heroes

These are the folks who must balance the daunting tasks of being parent, chief cook, house keeper, sanitation manager, child-care provider, and home arbiter of peace, all while working their regular 8-12-hour jobs.

These business and professional heroes are working to keep our economy alive & well to the best of their ability in the most difficult and challenging of times. Finding ways to keep small businesses up and running is key to the survival of our economy. Keeping in touch with the client base, helping them in creative ways, assures them of their own future in the market. Assurance equals confidence and confidence equals hope.

Helping people look at their work force differently and manage efficiently will give a shot of relief to the harried business managers.

All over our country teachers are using every tool they have in their education backgrounds to teach our children through computers. It has to take some dynamic heroes to keep entire classrooms of children and young adults interested and challenged. They don't have enough supplies. They don't have the luxury of movement in a classroom. They don't have enough resources at all and yet there they are, coaxing our children, challenging our young adults, using every possible thing they can think of to get the job done well. We are teaching our children in cramped spaces with no real control over the environment. And they are doing it well!

Much of the innovation they have created and repurposed will be valuable pieces of their educators' tool bags even after the school doors open.

In another corner there are heroes keeping our families intact body and soul, and our children soothed, while this invisible war is being fought on the front lines. Inventive ways to keep minds growing, learning and thinking are popping up all over social media. These are times that truly "try men's souls" and the family is the first line of defense for that. Guidance, discipline, love and care…the watchwords of parenting, are being highlighted in a way that hasn't happened in a long while. Quality time now meets quantity time and we are seeing benefits to that long term. Both parents and grandparents fill these roles. Stories of grandparents who care for their grandchildren while their own children work 8- and 12-hour days and nights, sometimes 6-7 days a week are the norm, not the exception now.

Just like the saying goes, "Not all heroes wear capes", I'm going to add another phrase, "Not all heroes save lives. Some save souls", including pastors, rabbis, priests, and all who serve the human soul. Where would be we without their counsel, their wisdom, and their willingness to provide services online for us in so many creative and meaningful ways.

And while America is cooking and baking again, we are also reading to our children more, walking our dogs more, seeing and smiling more at our neighbors, from a 6 ft distance. It seems like we know instinctively that we are all in the same boat and it's a lot easier when we are paddling in the same direction.

While we are using technology to its absolute extreme, we are also unplugging for the sake of sanity and our own best interests. Family taking care of family; Friends taking care of friends, all while operating under dire thoughts of what might be.

Some of our hidden heroes are sewing viable masks for everyone and some are designing new ways to fight the war behind the scenes. Some are inventing equipment needed for our front liners or for the critical testing that all of us need. Their efforts will help to expedite the end of this pandemic. Our volunteers are constantly busy creatively solving problems.

Scientists and research professionals will be working with an eye to the future…a 'life after the pandemic' scenario, on various ways health care delivery will change, as well as the many effects on other non-medical issues.

We look longingly toward the future and all the ways our lives will change because of what we have learned and how we have been challenged to do and think differently about things.

Life will go on and life will look incredibly different.

Great innovations are built out of great need. For every one of these critical jobs, we thank you for your sacrifices.

This piece is dedicated to all our heroes, yours and mine, who make a difference each and every day!

Who doesn't love a good hug, or a warm hand to hold, or someone to cuddle with?

Whether you are a hugger or not, most of us have a need to be together with those we love.

Outside your Pandemic Circle, however you have defined it, when was the last time you got close enough to hug someone?

It is either hard to recollect, or it is seared into your memory like the day of your first kiss.

The last normal hug for me was the middle of March, 2019, well before we were asked to Stay Safe and Stay at Home. And it was a banner day for me as I got to hug all 4 of my children and my 4-legged grand dog. My son's fiancé, Lu was returning to Amsterdam and had stopped with my son, Jared, to say goodbye. I held both Lu and Jared tightly. I breathe in every bit of them, and if I'm lucky, I can feel their hearts beat. I carry their warmth with me for a long time that way.

Earlier in the day I had seen my daughter, Kathryn, her husband, Josh and Pepper, their precious Tibetan Terrier. We always say goodbye with long hugs and lots of waving from the driveway, which includes the sign for "I love you" and some weird little wave, a finger wiggle, that I didn't know I did till my daughter mimicked it one evening. It has become a funny little endearment. Families are so weird and beautiful. God knew I would need that day of close and solid holding to get me through the next 6+ months. The very next day Ohio was on "lock down" with only a few exceptions. The word "essential" took on new meaning, along with other words that morphed into an entire lexicon of pandemic language.

We all have these significant moments seared into our minds now. They are the little treasures that hold big promises for us. And we crave them more than dark chocolate or Clorox clean-up wipes.

Things are different when you live alone. You don't have the built-in support system under the same roof that families and roommates provide, or loving human touch any time you need it.

But no matter if you live alone or with others, these are extraordinarily difficult times.

While we stay 6' apart, we will find a way to connect, a way to be together safely. We need each other more than ever. In the meantime, stay safe, sane and connected.

Rock of Ages

Written July 24, 2020

I've been painting a lot of rocks lately. I know that sounds crazy. But for me, the very act of holding a freshly clean, warm rock in my hands feels therapeutic.

As I turn the rock over and over again, I find balance while I find the exact place I want to paint. Or I paint all around the rock …so that any way you may place it in your windowsill or on your desk, there is something different to look at.

At first, I just painted words. I called them Pandemic words for Pandemic times. Words like: Trust, Adapt, Hope, Joy, Love, Peace, Faith, & Eternity (as in "this pandemic is lasting an eternity").

Later I added flowers on the bottom of the rock as a surprise. One flower became two or twelve.

It is amazing how much horror and sadness you can block with distractions. Rock painting was similar to Hallmark movie bingeing, with a little more purpose. As I painted each rock, I began to think of the people I would give the rock to. I began to think of them as rock solid symbols of survival during this world-wide pandemic. 2 rocks turned into 250 rocks, give or take, placed both purposely on porch steps and randomly wherever I went. My Hope Daisy rock became my signature igneous expression.

All of the rocks I painted fit on window sills, nightstands, in glove compartments, and in pockets. For the tactile among us, holding a rock in our hands provides comfort as daily we determine what our priorities are.

I have certainly run the gamut of Pandemic Distractions.

I have baked and delivered bread, cleaned out closets and cabinets, reorganized my garage to accommodate grocery disinfection along with mail and box cooling areas, made space for sanitizer, the rare wipes, and Clorox to clean large surfaces, not ingest. I have arranged my garage for winter "strategically-spaced" gatherings of family and friends.

I have made my half bathroom the mask cleaning & drying area. I have knitted in 90-degree weather, painted baseboards and spots on walls, sharpened knives, grown more flowers, tried to write in spits and starts, painted thin paper bookmarks & zoomed way too much.

But rock painting has remained my favorite by far. It has only been recently that I reluctantly cleared off my kitchen counter of all my painting supplies and my space on the floor for drying time. Sixteen months and 250+ rocks later, the intense rock painting period is over. I will paint every now and then. But it is time to move on and find another favorite way to manage the next phase of our pandemic crisis.

Why did I choose rocks in the first place? Because I am fascinated by them. My porch, my deck, my bedroom and living room all hold rocks I have gathered from various parts of the country...rocks I just cannot let out of my life.

Webster and my college Geology books say that rocks are "mineral matter of variable composition, assembled in nature by the action of heat or water". By their very nature, rocks are strong and enduring...just what we need to be today and every day.

Rivers have run over them, winds have blown around them, time and people have smashed their edges. But they are still here; still bringing weight and substance to the world.

They are the rocks of ages long ago and they remind me of the One Rock of Ages, the unwavering, unfailing source of strength, who will stand beside us all our lives, no matter how much the winds of fortune may whirl around us; no matter how frightening and upside down our world may become at times.

We have been put to the test with our own individual types of heat and water.

We are experiencing the heat of divisiveness, everywhere, the simmering heat of anxiety and depression. We are enduring the actual physical heat of a searing summer of record-breaking high temperatures; a lack of water in many areas and an excess of water in others.

We experience the heat of endless endurance of this Pandemic. The eternal ticking clock of time wears on us like a constant drip of water on our foreheads. We are many months in and some of us still have a hard time remembering what day it is. We still lack many things: space, supplies, activities, services, patience, and tolerance.

How can we remain strong in the face of these ultimate tests?

How can we withstand the pressure of heat and water?

We cannot afford the luxury of waiting for the "storm to pass". We must continue to find our way through.

We can feel the calm of His rock-steady Hand in our lives even while madness swirls around us. Even while!

Those are the rock-solid gifts we get and the ones we give.

Meanwhile, I unabashedly say ...Rock On!

When Justice Reigns

Written January 18, 2021

Since January 6, 2021, when our country's Democracy was threatened, there have been a lot of articles, sermons, and conversations across our nation, promoting peace.

Peace, love, and unity!

Those words from the 60's apply now in the 2020's.

But jumping straight to the position of peace without stopping on the corner of accountability, is too much of a shortcut for my thinking.

My regular compass and my moral compass take me on a journey with a bit more landscape in between.

America, after all, did not come to January 6, 2021 in one moment or in one giant step of discord.

We crept up to it year by year, lie by lie, wrongdoing by wrongdoing over the course of years, many, many years.

We allowed, along the way, missteps of injustice, unaccounted for crimes against humanity, and unyielding prejudices to become "normalized". In the end, we minimized the wrong things.

It starts with a little lie.

And when that lie is accepted and repeated over and over again from the top-down level, distrust is put into motion.

Confusion and chaos then step in to manage the circus of misinformation and disinformation. Once those who are watching see that this method works to fool the masses, then everyone gets in on the act.

Pretty soon, distrust is in full swing and the facts get mixed in with the little lies.

Bigger lies, the more important ones are born.

When truth is no longer respected and anything can be truth, we have lost control.

Timothy Snyder, in his book, "On Tyranny, 20 Lessons from the 20th Century", writes "To abandon facts is to abandon freedom. If nothing is true, then no one can criticize power, because there is no basis upon which to do so. If nothing is true, then all is spectacle. The biggest wallet pays for the most blinding lights."

We allow all that to happen every time we look the other way in order to keep the peace; or brush off blatant hypocrisy because we don't want to make waves; and every time we allow excuses to cloud our view of what is happening right before our very eyes. Every time we decide to "hold our tongues" because we don't want to upset anyone's sensibilities.

It is inconvenient to speak up!

There is no question that it is unpopular to speak out against something.

I know. I have been challenged for my words and had a text or post ignored because I am certain it made the receiver uncomfortable. I understand that. No one wants to feel uncomfortable. I find, however, that if I am feeling uncomfortable about something, it usually means that I need to take a second look, or take a closer look. But it doesn't mean I can look away.

It even feels uncomfortable to post this piece. I am almost certain it will have repercussions from some corners.

But I would rather stand for something I truly believe in and lose approval or even friends, than whitewash a message and lose who I am in the process.

I hold the same scrutiny over my own thoughts and actions that I hold for everyone else. I really don't believe in smoothing "things" over until the "things" have been buried, and forgotten. I am not one to stay silent while something has been misrepresented, while lies are spread. And I don't believe in sweeping things under the rug.

Have you taken a look under any rugs lately? I lifted up a big rug from my garage the other day and was appalled. There was a whole lot of filth and mess underneath, while all around it was pristine clean. We have to take that "rug" out in bright light and fresh air, and shake it silly till we get all the mess out.

To move forward after January 6, with any kind of common sense, we need to shake a few things out. We have to deal with the uncomfortable truth that maybe we have not seen something exactly as it is; or maybe we were not willing to give something up in order to right a wrong. We have to be willing to be uncomfortable, at the very least, in order to gain the peace we so desire.

We are a nation in need of accountability, justice and peace.

But "There is no shortcut to anywhere worth going".

Those are the words on the back of the compass necklace my daughter gave me.

They have applied in many things in my life since the day I fastened it around my neck as a constant reminder of not taking the easy way out of any problem. They apply now to our country.

We must do the hard thing now. The right thing to do is right before our eyes!

Let's take our rose-colored glasses off and replace them with laser sharp vision that sees the truth and values the future enough to do something about it.

Then and only then can we have peace!

Part Five:

What We Learn from Sacred Times

Lent: Change is Going to Come

When we learn something new our brains change. New connections and neurons are formed, pathways are strengthened, and our brains are never the same again.

When we fall in or out of love our lives are made different.

We make catastrophic mistakes that alter our thinking and our behavior.

We mend the edges of our personalities and we become something better.

Change happens whether we welcome it or not.

The season of Lent is all about mystery, mourning, unlikely partnerships, trials, loss and love, and a change so powerful that it rocked the world.

Lent tells us that change is going to come, the kind of change that alters our hearts and our thinking, readies us for the new, the exciting, the holy, and we are never the same again.

Revelations 21: 5
“Behold, I am making all things new.”

The Dichotomy of Jesus

I loved the word "dichotomy" before I knew the definition. I liked first how it sounded, bouncing off the roof of my mouth, and then what it meant. It seemed to describe and affirm my life so perfectly.

The "contrast between two seemingly opposing ideas, or existences" is exactly the sweet spot where I thrive. Even the most logical and ordered among us are prone to some degree of duality, or even a little whimsy at times.

None of us is a perfect straight line of action. Linear thinking isn't the only route.

Who among us has not been working on a healthy lifestyle, while nibbling on a Hershey Kiss here and there? Why can't we both embrace the logic of algebra and also love the satisfaction of alliteration?

And who doesn't hike for two hours, then bask in a lounge chair, reading a good book?

I pulled my grocery list off of the refrigerator this morning and examined it carefully before entering the contents into Kroger Curbside. And that's when it hit me again. Yep, I live a life full of dichotomy.

Marching in a straight line as if they all belonged logically together, are items that make up a puzzling grocery list.

Partial evidence is offered below:

Salmon
Hot dogs
Spinach
Butter
Blueberries
Hershey Kisses
Wine
Toothpaste

If I have to point out the contradictions, then you are definitely one of my Tribe!

Come visit me. Bring your colorful thinking and we'll bask in the crazy conversation of zigzag minds!

Lists that confound; patterns with seeming dichotomies; paradoxical thinking remind me of who Jesus was when He walked on earth.

Everything about Him is a contrast and an exercise in paradox.

Born in a stable, born to be King!

I love the "table turning" Jesus as much as I love the Jesus who said "Bring the children unto me". The Jesus who cares enough to shepherd one lost sheep even though He has just saved hundreds on a hillside.

He was and is the merciful Savior who gave His life so we could live it. A living-dying contradiction.

His message of "Love is the Answer" alongside "Crucifixion on the Cross" equals the Paradise Paradox.

Jesus teaches that we have to embrace the illogical to truly understand His life of sacrifice.

Concepts like, "We triumph through defeat"; "We lead by serving"; "We believe concretely in the unseen" are all seeming contradictions.

If we can embrace change, then we are better able to receive the wonders of divine dichotomy.

Some of us come reluctantly to that, some receive it immediately.

Either way, when we are at home with all sides of Jesus, we can accept that two different things can be true at the same time, for we are never just "ONE" thing at a time. And this makes ALL things possible.

2 Corinthians 12:10
"For when I am weak, then I am strong."

Matthew 10:39
"Whoever finds his life will lose it, and whoever loses his life for my sake will find it."

The Mystery Unfolds: Maunday Thursday

It was just an ordinary Thursday and yet it was the beginning of the end of the beginning.

The unlikely washing of feet; the feast of wine and bread; the prophesies of betrayal; the mystery message of the body and the cup; the lesson of the "greatest"; the unheeded warnings...So many extraordinary things happened on an ordinary Thursday.

Jesus is the master of the unexpected.

He came to turn the tables on our lives and upend expectations.

His coming changed all our impossibles to possible and our ordinary to extraordinary.

When I think of all he accomplished during the short time He had on earth, I realize that everything He did, He did with intention and purpose. His actions matched his words and his words were powerful. "Love your neighbor as yourself." "Blessed are the merciful." "You are the light of the world." "Come and follow me." "...do not be like the hypocrites." "Do not judge." "Come to me all you who are weary, and I will give you rest." "Forgive." "Watch, wait and pray."

On this Maundy Thursday, take some time to consider the hope of the Impossible Possible.

Ponder what it means to be the least; and what it means to betray.

Think about the gift of the Cup…that overflows for us.

Take a moment to imagine the sacrifice and sacrificial love that He freely gave!

Maundy Thursday comes to us just when we think we can take no more, when we think it cannot get any worse. It comes and causes us to stop in our tracks and take stock.

On a ledger sheet of debits and credits, we come to the table wanting.

We come to the table less than humble and yet He gives us the chance to get it right; to know that He is the one who can provide the way out of our debt, the way out of darkness.

What is asked of us in return?

To humble ourselves, acknowledge who is king, and offer our vulnerable hearts as we wait to receive His unexpected, over-the-top offering.

Wait, yet another "hour".

The dark is here, now.

But the Light is coming.

Breathe in the hope that comes even in the darkest days.

Matthew 26: 1-35; Mark 14: 12-31; Luke 22:7-38; John 13: 1-38

Love Made a Way: Good Friday

If you knew you had only hours left on this earth before you would die the most unjust, horrific death, what would you do in those hours?

Defend yourself against those who have wrongly accused you and intend to do you fatal harm?

Try to escape and run for your life?

Make a bargain with the devil to live no matter what?

Drink a potion to numb the impending pain and agony?

We're human, we might do any of those or anything else, except what Jesus did.

Jesus did none of those things.

In fact, His last hours were spent in constant pain and agony up until the end.

This day, Good Friday, is considered the darkest day, for good reason.

Jesus experienced all that is the worst of being human. Why? Why did that happen?

He could have taken the easy way out. He was God after all.

But that was not the plan of the Father.

God knew we needed a Savior who could understand our every pain, our every betrayal, and our own feelings of being betrayed, our worst nightmares become real.

He knew we needed a Savior who could have saved himself but chose to save us instead. Sacrificial love became the culmination of Jesus' work on earth, the hardest work imaginable.

And because He was still holy as he was still human, He felt every sin that had ever been committed in history up to that point and to the point beyond...of future time, for all of us, and all to come. That burden is an unbearable one, and yet He bore it for us. He knew we would need him to understand our frailties, our very humanness.

If there were ever an act that said "YOU MATTER", Good Friday was that for us, for all time. In all our trials, in all our sorrows, even in all our ugliness and sins, we matter to our Savior. We matter to God! Love came down to be sacrificial love for us! We needed a God who could be "with us", Emmanuel for us. It is hard to get our minds around that kind of selflessness. But that love is for us...that amazing gift is for us.

We needed Him to "know" and still to love us. Isn't that what we all crave...To have someone in our lives who knows the very essence of us, good and bad, and still believes in us, still understands, still cares, still loves all of us?

The path that Jesus would have taken as he carried his cross to crucifixion on Good Friday, is called Via Dolorosa, "the way of suffering", "the way of sorrows".

On that darkest of days, down that dark road, and up on that dark cross, Jesus gave it all for us, every single one of us, no exceptions, we are ALL offered that kind of love.

He came to fulfill the law…to make the Law of Love the most important commandment of all.

For when it was done, when all the betrayals were committed by friends and foes, when all the atrocities were committed against Him, when he saved the soul of the man on the cross beside him even when He was dying Himself, when all the insults had been hurled against Him, when the words, "It is finished" were spoken *(John 19: 30)* …at that very moment, "the curtain of the temple was torn in two from top to bottom". *(Mark 15: 38)*

"The earth shook and the rocks split. The tombs broke open…" *(Matthew 27: 51-52)*. And the law was finally fulfilled as the Law of Love!

It was, indeed, the darkest day…but God left us even in that day, a ray of hope, the promise that we no longer needed an intercessory for us with Him. We now had a straight line to our Savior, to our God.

"Love has made a way. Hope is never lost. There's power in the Cross." From "Power in the Cross", by Derek Johnson.

There's more of course, much more.

And so we wait…we watch and wait for the rest of the story.

The Trial and Power of Waiting: Holy Saturday

Twiddling my thumbs, pacing the floor, I find myself waiting once again. I've spent far too many hours like this.

Waiting for the letter or the apology that is long overdue.

Waiting for the diagnosis we dread.

Waiting for the right person, the right job to show up in our lives.

Waiting for the news NOT to contain the words COVID, war, poverty or 'senseless' anything.

Waiting for the jury to decide.

Waiting for your life to begin again.

Waiting for the darkness to recede.

For the sun to rise.

How much time?

We wait so much; you would think we would be experts by now.

Instead, we don't seem to have much to show for it. It takes its toll in our emotional health.

We don't have to live that way...at least we don't have to linger so long.

What if we did something positive while we waited and we traded negative thoughts for trusting ones?

Some things and people were meant to exit our lives, even though we may have been holding on for dear life.

Some jobs were meant to be left in order to provide the space for a better career.

Some trials were not meant to harm, but to sharpen and mold us to become a stronger, more enlightened self.

What if our best mindset would be to sit still and wait without the backdrop of negativity.

What if we knew we were never alone while we wait.

What if we thought of waiting less like a trial, something to be endured and more like an expectation in the middle of chaos. An expectation of hope, that brings the gift of calm and peace, isn't that what trust really is?

What power would come from that kind of waiting!

There is power in trusting that good will triumph over evil; that love will reign over hate; that life will prevail and victory will triumph over death.

Yes, that is what the Saturday between Good Friday and Easter is about...waiting, watching, trusting.

Is the wait worth it? Oh, my, yes...it is worth every moment!

Spend your "Saturdays" in watchful faith, knowing you are not alone, knowing for certain that God reigns; that He is present in every single moment, especially the silent ones, ready and waiting to burst into praise!

Psalm 130: 5
"I wait for the Lord, my soul waits,
And in His word, I put my hope."

A Time to Mourn and a Time to Pray: Holy Saturday

Holy Saturday...a time of watching and waiting.

Forty hours of watching and waiting during an already tumultuous time. I picture a sunless sky, air thick with unsettling strife, bodies covered and faces hidden by cloth in fear. Minds filled with fear of retribution for following Jesus, fear of being caught by the Roman guards, fear of the unknown. It's an unsettling kind of prolonged quiet.

That's what I imagine when I think of the Marys, Mary, the mother of Jesus, Mary Magdeline, and Mary of Clopas, waiting somewhere near and grieving for Jesus.

One thing is clear. They were believers. Followers of Jesus all through the 3 years of his mission on earth, they walked with him from Galilee to Jerusalem to the cross and stayed close by until the very end. They were not going to forsake him now.

Their faithfulness would later allow them to be in the right place at the right time to become the earliest "witnesses" for Christ.

At least that's how I look at their last recorded important role.

Waiting near the tomb would be a dangerous place to wait. The Roman soldiers were there overseeing the stone in front of Jesus' tomb, making certain His disciples did not roll it away and steal Jesus from the tomb. No wonder they might have been afraid. That didn't drive them away in defeat. No, they watched and waited.

Courage, commitment, and radical love compelled the women to risk much to be there or close by.

The Bible mentions the word "wait" and other forms of the word hundreds of times. I stopped counting at 108, enough to deduce the emphasis God places on waiting. However, if you are equating the word "wait" with standing still and twiddling your thumbs, reroute your thinking, please.

God's kind of waiting is not to be misconstrued with doing nothing.

What do you think the Marys were doing while they were "waiting on the Lord"?

Praying, pondering, mourning, remembering, honoring...whatever it is that they were doing or feeling, I am certain it was done with a concentrated focus on Jesus.

Imagine what we could accomplish if we approached every prayer request with that kind of zeal and persistence.

Yes, we will "fall asleep" on the job at times. But when we commit to powerful prayer, powerful things happen!

When we partner with God, He is at work while we are waiting and praying.

He is always on watch! He never sleeps, never dozes, never stops or strays from His plan.

To be bold, to risk everything, to pray with conviction, knowing the answers may not be what we had hoped for, that is faith.

The Marys knew this and were rewarded.

But that happens later when the sun rises on the triumphant Risen Son!

And so, we watch and wait. Sunday is coming!

The Power and the Glory: Easter Sunday

He has Risen!

He has Risen Indeed!

Those words are the welcomed "Call and Answer" for Christians around the globe every Easter Sunday.

I say those words out loud and I text them over and over every Easter morning. The pure delight in seeing either one of those phrases from a family member or dear friend when I open my phone, is enough to make my day each and every time. That's what it's like to believe, to know!

But long ago when it happened for the very first time, it was in fact unbelievable to the women who arrived at the tomb early that first Easter morning, to find the stone rolled away and Jesus gone from the tomb.

They ran to tell this news to the disciples.

It was just as incredulous to Peter and John, the two disciples who arrived next, to check to see if the nonsense the women had told them was true. They knew Jesus had died and were convinced he was never coming back. That would be unbelievable.

Unbelievable… and yet, the proof was staring them in the face: the absence of the body of Jesus, the strips of linen cloths and the burial cloth that had been wound around Jesus's head, folded up and placed in a separate spot from the linen cloths.

There is a little more to the story.

When Peter and John ran to the tomb, John got there first, but did not enter the tomb. He waited at the entrance as he looked inside. Peter arrived and ran straight into the tomb, looking around as well. They both saw the same things. Luke says that Peter left, "wondering to himself what had happened". Later Peter founded the church at Antioch and then became the head of the church in Rome. Peter was known as "the Rock". He wrote 1st and 2nd Peter. Next John entered the tomb. John 20: 8 says, "Finally the other disciple, who had reached the tomb first, also went inside. He saw and believed." John became a leader in the church and went on to write both the book of John and Revelations.

Two different reactions to the same evidence. Just like in today's world.

John went back to his home, but Mary Magdalene, who had remained close by the tomb, began to cry, as she had thought that the Romans had taken Jesus's body away. She wept and looked into the tomb and saw two angels sitting where Jesus' body had been. They asked her why she was crying and she told them. She turned around and saw Jesus standing there, but she didn't recognize him. He asked her again who she was looking for and she answered.

Then He said her name… "Mary". And she knew.

She knew His voice when He called her name.

There is a tender scripture in the Bible that tells us the sheep know their shepherd's voice. It's in John 10:27, "My sheep listen to my voice; I know them, and they follow me."

What was said between them next, between Jesus, the Savior of the World and his faithful Mary Magdalene, is recorded in John 20: 17-18 "…Go to my brothers and tell them, I am returning to my Father and your Father, to my God and your God."

"Mary Magdalene went to the disciples with the news: ***'I have seen the Lord!'***"

Could she have been the first Christian witness?

No matter if it was the first or the "first-hundredth", it was a powerful witness on a powerful day.

It makes me think of one of my favorite Easter Sunday songs:

"Christ the Lord is Risen Today" by Charles Wesley in 1739.

Christ the Lord is risen today. Alleluia!
Sons of men, and angels say. Alleluia!
Raise your joys and triumphs high. Alleluia!
Sing, ye heavens, and earth reply. Alleluia!

Love's redeeming work is done. Alleluia!
Fought the fight, the battle's won. Alleluia!
Death in vain forbids him rise! Alleluia!
Christ has opened paradise. Alleluia!

There's so much more to the story, but this is the main event, the battle won!

This is the hope we have in Him.

The rest of the story is left in our hands. What do we do with that news once we have heard it? Do we walk away unmoved, or walk away and ponder; or do we let it immediately change our hearts and cause us to share the news with any who will listen?

What does our own Alleluia sound like on this Easter Sunday?

Advent Season:
Big Promises, Bigger Gifts!

Introduction:

The book of Luke is full of God's Promises and His incredible gifts.

Looking at the story of Christ through the eyes of Paul's dear friend, Luke, the physician, shows us God's love, mercy and instruction for our lives. I think God chose Luke to write this gospel because, in addition to his thoroughness, he was an endearing person with qualities we all can relate to. He was a loyal friend to Paul when others had deserted him. He was a physician, who healed the body and so very much wanted to be a part of Christ's healing of the soul. He was a detailed professional and an exacting truth teller. And he saw the greater picture that God had in mind.

Luke wrote this book in part to 'displace disconnected and ill-founded reports about Jesus'.

He passionately wanted us to know the TRUTH of Jesus!

He wrote it for **ALL** believers, as well as for those who would read and **THEN** believe.

He wrote thoroughly and knowledgeably to assure that we **"know the certainty"** of God's Word. (Luke 1:1-4) And so he used his own talents and skills as a doctor to be **believable**; to get to the ***truth*** and the ***heart of the matter***.

My hope is that these devotions get to the "truth" and the "heart of the matter" for any who would read them and that you be led to uncover promises of your own from the good doctor, a faithful follower of Christ.

Certainty in an Uncertain World

Luke 1: 19   "I am Gabriel. I stand in the presence of God, and I have been sent to you to tell you this good news."

Luke 1: 28   "Greetings, you who are highly favored! The Lord is with you."

The appearance of the angel of the Lord, Gabriel, to two people: Zechariah and Mary, the mother of Jesus, is an attention-grabbing way to start the book of Luke! That's what I call a power play by God.

Gabriel's first words were, "I am Gabriel. I stand in the presence of God'.

Aren't those awe-inspiring words? The power behind them sends chills through me every single time I read them.

Can you imagine being given a message from an angel who says that he "stands in the presence of God"? Can we even imagine what that might feel like, or what his voice would be like?

No wonder he has to tell both Zechariah and Mary not to be afraid. I imagine Gabriel as a compelling, majestic being, with a voice so moving and dramatic that not even Charlton Heston, as Moses in The Ten Commandments, could adequately portray that kind of commanding charisma.

And when he says he stands in the presence of God, certainly that would be credentials enough for me to believe him. But would it really have been enough? For me? For you?

Even, the priest, Zechariah, well into his senior years, struggled with this message from God. Gabriel tells old

Zechariah that he and Elizabeth are going to have a baby whose name will be called, John. Gabriel lays it all out in great detail, what John's divine mission in life will be, and it's a pretty big, God-sized mission.

But Zechariah reacted with such disbelief that Gabriel silenced his doubts by taking away his voice until Zechariah's son, John the Baptist, was born many months later.

It wasn't until the relatives were going to name the baby after his father, that Zechariah found his voice and said, "No, his name is John".

Those simple words were his redeeming testimony to belief.

Talk about making the best of second chances! Zechariah had his second chance and went on to proclaim his faith in a glorious song of his own that stands the test of time. Read it in Luke 1: 67-79.

Mary's question to Gabriel had more to do with the implementation rather than the certainty of the plan itself. Her confident words, "I am the Lord's servant. May it be to me as you have said" along with her impactful words in Mary's Song, Luke 1:46-55, exhibit a faith and belief well beyond her teen-age years!

Yes, this first chapter of Luke, with its 80 verses, is a powerful chapter indeed!

With all the benefit of history, we think we would believe easily if God sent an angel to give us a message. Surely, we would know it by the startling appearance of an angel like Gabriel. His voice alone would convince us. And those powerful words!

But in reality, trust has never been a plentiful commodity in our world, and most of us need more proof the message is from God, Himself.

A lot of us are veritable, doubting Zechariahs and Thomases.

Most of us are really not like Mary at all.

We want a guarantee, a life-time warranty.

And that's why He sent us Jesus…a Messenger from God, so Holy, so full of Truth, so close to the presence of God, as to BE God, in the Trinity!

He knew we needed the Son of God **and** the Son of man.

On this first day of Advent, we prepare our hearts to accept the Wonder of Christ!

We have been given this Promise, this warranty, made for all humanity for all the ages:

That we are loved so much that God would give His Son to us and for us, to be **with** us forever!

What a Promise that is! What a Gift Divine!

Prayer:

Jesus, our Hope for all ages,

As we seek the certainty of You in our lives, help us be assured of the truth in your Word; the depth of your love and the breadth of your promises.

Open our hearts to receive your gifts with gratitude and faith. Amen.

Elizabeth and the Mighty Power of the Holy Spirit

Luke 1: 36-45

How did I miss it?

How did I miss this important implication in the first chapter of Luke? Granted Luke packed at least 500 sermons in his book, and about 100 of them are in chapter one. Still, I missed this critical piece until today.

Luke 1:35-45. Read it and let all the amazing promises of God settle into your heart and mind.

(This is the angel Gabriel speaking right after he has surprised her with a visit and given her the news that she will be the mother of God's son. Mary has a logical question to ask: "How can this be since I am a virgin?")

"The angel, Gabriel, answered, "The holy Spirit will come upon you, and the power of the Most High will overshadow you. So, the holy one to be born will be called the Son of God.

"Even Elizabeth your relative is going to have a child in her old age, and she who was said to be barren, is in her 6th month. For nothing is impossible with God."

"I am the Lord's servant," Mary answered. "May it be to me as you have said." Then the angel left her.

At that time Mary got ready and hurried to a town in the hill country of Judea, where she entered Zechariah's home and greeted Elizabeth. When Elizabeth heard Mary's greeting, the baby leaped in her womb, and Elizabeth was filled with the Holy Spirit.

In a loud voice she exclaimed, "Blessed are you among women, and blessed is the child you will bear! But why am I so favored, that the mother of my Lord should come to me? As soon as the sound of your greeting reached my ears, the baby in my womb leaped for joy. Blessed is she who has believed that what the Lord has said to her will be accomplished."

There are only 10 verses in this passage but they are power-packed with God's promises and God's principles.

Let's go back to this ancient time and place and see if we can imagine ourselves in this scene. Mary has been visited by the arch angel Gabriel, the one that God often uses to communicate the most important messages of all. He has proclaimed some powerful news that directly affects her and the rest of her life. At the tender age of about 13, Mary has accepted this news with the poise and elevated faith of someone far older and wiser. She was unbelievably mature. She was exactly who God thought she was.

The minute Gabriel left her, she packs her bags and heads out for a road trip to her relative Elizabeth. She went seeking her support person. Now we don't know this at all, but I like to imagine that Elizabeth was her favorite cousin. I like to think of them as kindred souls. You can imagine this any way you wish. But this version works for me, especially since I have my own special Elizabeth in my life, my cousin, Betsy. She too is wise, kind, loving and supportive. She is the friend who drives the extra 500 miles in a pandemic to be by another friend's side when she needed her most. She is THAT friend. So, I'm very biased to this name. Read it as you like, but God created THIS Elizabeth to figure in Mary's life in a big way! And He created Elizabeth as the one to teach the rest of us a few lessons as well.

Notice in one long action-packed sentence Luke has Mary leaving her own home, traveling to Judea, and immediately entering the home of Zechariah and Elizabeth. I think she was in a rush. I think she needed to talk this over with someone she trusted. And I think she needed more than one holy sleep over to do this.

Enter Mary into Elizabeth's home. No fanfare, just Mary's greeting. Maybe she said, "Hello! Elizabeth, it's Mary! Anybody home?" Mary is young, I imagine her voice as melodic. I think she is a soprano. By contrast, the older Elizabeth's voice is probably deeper...perhaps an alto. None of this is in Luke. It's just in my imagination but bear with me and go with it for a minute as I attempt to make a point.

This much we know for certain: Mary greets Elizabeth, (drumroll here) and the baby in Elizabeth's womb leaps for joy! That baby of course is the future John the Baptist, preparer of The Way. At that very moment of baby John's leaping for joy, Luke makes a point of telling us that Elizabeth was filled with the Holy Spirit. Filled!

In my own bible I underlined those very words years and years ago. Important then, important now. Only now, I see more clearly their meaning!

Luke notes that Elizabeth exclaimed "...in a loud voice, "Blessed are you among women, and blessed is the child you will bear."

But what Elizabeth says next is what my brain has glossed over for decades. She continues with this question, "But why am I so favored that the mother of my Lord should come to me?"

BINGO! She knew! Elizabeth KNEW!

Elizabeth knew exactly who this baby was and who this baby was going to grow up to be. She called Mary "the mother of my Lord".

This is amazing because:

- She didn't even know Mary was pregnant yet.
- There were no cell phones, no rotary dial phones, certainly no computers, no telegrams, not even Morse Code had been invented.
- Gabriel had not visited Elizabeth that day, as far as we know.
- And, finally, Elizabeth's own husband, Zechariah wasn't able to tell her because Gabriel had silenced him over 6 months ago, for a temporary moment of unbelief. How's that for a significant consequence?

But Elizabeth knew and Elizabeth believed! In a BIG way!

Despite the fact that later, after John is born, Zechariah "ups his game" and more than makes up for that temporary loss of faith, this is still a huge contrast of the two.

So now the question is: HOW did Elizabeth know?

The answer is given right there in those 10 verses.

The Holy Spirit.

The Holy Spirit and indisputable Faith had come washing over Elizabeth in one big incredible God moment. No wonder she exclaimed in a loud voice. I would have shouted it from thatched rooftops myself, had I been her.

This makes me wonder. Was Elizabeth one of the first (after Elisha and Mary) to experience the power of the Holy Spirit?

She knew and recognized Mary's unborn baby as the Savior of mankind, her Lord. That would imply discernment, a gift of the Holy Spirit. And it was an instantaneous gift.

One moment she was Elizabeth, an old woman, 6 months pregnant, maybe resting in her rocker. The next she was Elizabeth, mother of John the Baptist, crying out in a loud voice that this baby, that Mary was carrying, was the Lord of the Universe, the Rock of our Salvation!

And of course, this makes me wonder some more and ask myself some hard questions:

- Just how seriously do we take the Holy Spirit today?
- What things do we miss by ignoring God's holy nudges?
- What gifts of the Holy Spirit do we unwittingly keep under wraps?
- What moments of sharing God's Word and His Promises do we let pass us by?
- What joyful opportunities do we forfeit when we trudge through each day with the attitude of boredom or lack of purpose?
- Are we too afraid of commitment to forge meaningful relationships that will lead to spiritual connections?
- Are we too busy with the mundane to catch the mystical whispers of the Holy Spirit?
- Who needs us right now in their lives?

This is not a guilt trip down "regrets only" lane. But this is a wakeup call for me and maybe for you too.

So much emphasis is on God, our Father and Jesus, our Savior…and rightfully so!

But God in His wisdom planned for a Trinity. Jesus gave us the third gift of the Holy Spirit to be our Counselor here on earth.

The Holy Spirit is the One who is inside of us, whispering holy thoughts and urging us along our path of discipleship. He helps us realize our purpose on earth. When I recognize this gift as the magnitude of glory it really is, I fall on my knees in utter gratitude. And I rise again to listen.

What is He telling me today? What is His message for me?

This Christmas, and every day, let's get in tune with the Holy Spirit. Let's put on our best "Elizabeth eyes and ears". Let's be the voice who welcomes those who come into our homes, our Zooms, and our circles of influence and embrace all that they are and all that we know they can be.

Can you just see Elizabeth with Mary, holding hands as they walk that universal pregnant walk, talking and whispering holy secrets.

Can you hear Elizabeth encouraging Mary as she figures out how to tell Joseph this news?

Can you hear their anticipatory joy at being mothers together?

Can you hear all the angst Mary might have about raising the Son of God? Can you hear Elizabeth's faith-filled, loving responses?

The world needs more Elizabeths in it!

Let's remember her last words in verse 45...

"Blessed is she who has believed that what the Lord has said to her will be accomplished."

That's the faith of someone who has listened to the words of the Holy Spirit and accepted them as Truth!

Prayer:

Holy Father, in all your wisdom You knew exactly what we would need. The Holy Trinity was and still is the perfect plan. We need you. We need Jesus. And we need the Holy Spirit in our lives, every moment in every situation.

We need ALL of the wonders of You. Let it be so. Amen!

Out of the Mouths of Babes!

Luke 2: 48-49, 51 "When his parents saw him, they were astonished. His mother said to him, 'Son, why have you treated us like this? Your father and I have been anxiously searching for you.' *"Why were you searching for me?"* Jesus asked. *"Didn't you know I had to be in my Father's house?"*

"Then he went down to Nazareth with them and was obedient to them. But his mother treasured all these things in her heart."

Parenting is hard! It was hard even for the holy family.

It might be particularly hard for us during the holidays. Take heart! God has a plan for this!

I was glad to have good role models when I was first parenting, but all that wonderful advice would sometimes leave me feeling less than adequate and a bit out of sorts. Even though we know there is no such thing as perfect parenting, every mom and dad feels that unhealthy guilt of not living up to the standards we set for ourselves.

I found a soothing benefit from the parents who were willing to admit their infallibilities as well as their successes. We discussed bedtime routines, sleep schedules, food fusses, and the best toys for the best price. Mostly, we just shared one-pot recipes and muddled through alone.

Sometimes sound advice would come from an unexpected corner in our own homes: the words our children shared. And if we listened closely to these surprise gifts, they became golden, the times we grew in wisdom as parents. Some of my best lessons were learned from my mistakes and from listening to my own children.

I humbly submit to you an example from about 25 years ago.

Use your imagination and scroll back in time to the week of Halloween, sometime in the 90's.

On an otherwise lovely day in October, when my daughter was around 4 years old, she ran into the house, clearly upset and on the verge of tears. Her friend down the street (we'll call her Julie) had told her if she dressed up for Halloween and went trick or treating, the devil would find her and take her away. WHAT? What child would say such a thing? I couldn't have heard her correctly. But after a tearful repeat, the story was the same. And now my daughter thought she could not go Trick or Treating with her friends. After all, no one wants to get snatched up by the devil, especially while wearing your absolute favorite costume of all time.

To get a sense of why this was the favorite costume, it is important to note that in previous years I had cobbled together homemade costumes for her and her big brother. And while those were fun, this year, she would be wearing a store-bought dress, the dress of Beauty and the Beast character, Belle. She was beyond excited.

Her idea of trick or treating was to run as fast as she could from home to home in our neighborhood, ring the doorbell and wait expectantly for each neighbor to exclaim over her costume, offer the requisite candy, and praise her for her good manners. But THIS year, she was going to be wearing a glittery yellow-gold Belle dress! She could hardly wait for Trick or Treat night! Her pillow case and running shoes were already in place by the front door.

However, now, after Julie's words, my daughter was despondent that Halloween was not going to happen for her...

the year of "Belle" no less. She was also beside herself with fear of being "taken" by the devil when she stepped foot outside.

It was hard for me to think of another child actually saying the words "the devil will take you away" to my 4-year-old. How could Julie's parents tell her these despicable things? They spoke frequently about being Christians, and yet, Julie's words, which most likely came from them, were anything but Christ-like. Even though some controlled rage was powering my heartbeat into well above a healthy place, I held my tongue about Julie's words and thought I was managing this situation fairly well so far.

But my daughter, who could read the nuances of my countenance like the expert observer she was, knew this was NOT her mama's normal face.

(Luke 6:45 and Matthew 12:34 will tell you why she saw what she saw in my face.)

She looked at me and asked "Why are you looking that way? Your face is different. Are you mad at Julie, mommy?"

"I'm just wondering why in the world Julie would say those things to you. Sweetheart, everything is going to be ok. Nothing like that will happen to you on Halloween or any day. We will be with you at every house and you will be safe to run and have fun. There is nothing to worry about."

Ok, crisis averted! I thought my response to her worked, maybe even it was somewhere close to a perfect response. (NOPE! Close, but no cigar!)

God had a different "take" on this matter and a VERY different definition of "perfect".

God was concerned with my own heart right then, and its literal overflow to my face! The face my daughter was staring at so earnestly.

And then I was brought up short from my daughter's next words to me:

"Well, mommy, Jesus loves Julie just as much as He loves me. So, we have to forgive her."

You know that feeling when your own words come back to hit you right in the heart and make you look in the mirror of your sorry soul? Well, that was one of those moments for me.

Her words tore through the layer of my unkind thoughts, piercing me with conviction.

Wisdom from a 4-year-old who knew what the point was in this whole situation.

Point being: Jesus loves us ALL! He loves and redeems the ones who tell horrible things to their little friends; He loves and changes the hearts of parents who stand in judgment against those who hurt their children. Check!

Sometimes, as parents, it's best to "ponder in our hearts" from the perspective of His merciful grace rather than from the perspective of perceived parental perfection, which truly, none of us will ever have any way.

His Grace and His Mercy are best reflected in our lives, our words, and on our faces. We can't do that alone. So, we have Jesus...a few friends, and the little children that He loved so dearly, to help us through.

He doesn't ask for perfection. He asks for changed hearts, willing attitudes, and a sincere effort to align our hearts with our thoughts and our words...all coated heavily in Grace.

These are the **perfect gifts** He gives to us, sometimes out of the mouths of babes!

Prayer:

Lord Jesus, Redeemer of all, change our hearts. Help us listen to your voice. Help us receive conviction with graciousness and view it as a gift for our own good. Help us not to expect perfection from ourselves, our children, or any others, but rather to "grow in wisdom and stature, and in favor with God and man".

Amen.

Be Prepared!

Luke 3: 4-6; 10

"A voice of one calling in the desert, prepare ye the way for the Lord, make straight paths for him. Every valley shall be filled in, every mountain and hill made low. The crooked roads shall become straight, the rough ways smooth. And all mankind will see God's salvation."

"'What should we do then?', the crowd asked."

I can't read that passage without thinking of two things:

Thing One, the musical GODSPELL.

"PRE-E-E-PARE YE the way of the Lord! Pre-e-e-pare Ye the Way OF THE LORD.

I was thrilled in my 20's to be cast in Godspell. I was teaching high school at that time and also involved in the local community theater group. Godspell was one of my favorite musicals and the director, Mike Simons, was an incredibly talented man transplanted from New York. He was a Jewish man, directing a play about the power of Christ! His perspective was poignant and unique. Every time we entered the theater and sang in full voice, it felt like we were singing directly to God and for all of humanity.

Thing Two, I think of the Scouts of America! Boys and Girls! Wholesome youth, leading the way by their own timeless motto: BE PREPARED!

This motto has undoubtedly saved millions of lives in its time. The Scouts have it right in many things, but in this one, they are bright star leaders.

Be prepared...plain and simple advice. What does it mean? What is expected?

If you are in Scouting, you will work on skills that will teach you how to survive both in the wilderness and in the real world. That work will cause you to become a well-rounded person and citizen of the world.

Even if you are not in Scouting, you can recognize that their motto, Be Prepared, is good advice that keeps us on our toes, skillfully navigating life.

Scouts learn to be prepared for any situation.

Be prepared as if your life depends on it.

In the case of the mission of John the Baptist, lives did depend on it, worldly lives and eternal ones.

John was the son of Zechariah (of Devotion #1) and Elizabeth, and he was called "John, the Baptist", because his mission was to baptize as many as he could. His was a baptism of repentance and forgiveness of sins.

And just to make sure the crowds knew the difference, he constantly told them that he "baptized with water", but the "One more powerful" than he would come and baptize with "fire and the Holy Spirit."

People were faithful to John, probably because he was so sincere, so focused on his mission, so faithful to the One he knew was coming to save us. He didn't care what he wore, where he lived or what he ate. He lived only to prepare the way for Christ to come and be recognized by all who saw and all who believed.

This was big news! The crowds were numerous. The crowds were faithful.

John's "branding" back then was the phrase: "Prepare the Way for the Lord!"

Can you see him coming out of the wilderness, shouting those words? Can you hear the conviction in his voice? His followers must have felt that same urgency, to do whatever it takes to "prepare the way for the Lord".

They hungered to know more so they asked him, "What should we do then?"

This is the question of the ages. What should we do to be prepared for Jesus?

And then the follow up question: What should we do next?

Jesus pares it down and makes it simple for us to understand and to do:

3 things and a follow up question.

1. I acknowledge my sins.
2. I ask for forgiveness.
3. I proclaim and believe the words: Jesus is the son of God. He is my Savior.

John was finally able to realize his ultimate mission, the baptism of Jesus. And that was the moment when Jesus was forever tied to God and the Holy Spirit, the moment that acknowledged Jesus' position in the Trinity.

"As Jesus was being baptized and He was praying, the heavens opened and the Holy Spirit descended on him and a voice came from heaven: "You are my Son, whom I love; with you I am well pleased." (Verse 22)

Once we accept that sacred connection to God, our lives are forever changed.

It's not required for salvation, but it's the fulfilling act that enriches our lives and spreads the good news to others.

The follow up: Now that we know...how then do we live?

Prayer: *Savior of my soul and Hope of my heart, prepare my life so that it is a light that shines in the world! Prepare me to make an eternal difference! Amen.*

Jesus, and the Ultimate Purpose Driven Life

Luke 4: 42-44

"At daybreak Jesus went out to a solitary place. The people were looking for him and when they came to where he was, they tried to keep him from leaving them. But he said, "I must preach the good news of the kingdom of God to the other towns also, because that is why I was sent." And he kept on preaching in the synagogues of Judea."

It's now the 4th chapter of Luke and I imagine you're thinking this devotional is going to be about the temptation of Jesus, or the prophet not being accepted in his own hometown because those verses are typically the big choices. This time when I read chapter 4, another choice jumped up and caught my attention.

What are your plans for Christmas? What list is on your fridge or in your planner today? In early December the lists start piling up. You know which ones: the gift lists, the holiday meals' grocery lists, decoration and party planning lists, church committee lists, the untangle and hang the lights list, the extended family white elephant gift list, and the "order ASAP" list.

You're probably in the midst of "checking your lists once, twice" scribbling on them until they're hardly recognizable. That observation was for the "pencil and paper" folks. To the other very efficient people with device lists somewhere in that mysterious 'cloud', I hope you too find the satisfaction of checking off items.

Sadly, those lists, whatever form they take, may represent a workload dragging us down the road of physical exhaustion and mental weariness, robbing us of the very parts of Christmas we hold sacred. We work ourselves into a frenzy. We become cranky, crabby, cantankerous, maybe even resentful. What, you exclaim! Resentful of Christmas? It has been known to happen.

Too many lists and too little time to get it done may find you hiding out from Christmas. That panicked, cornered feeling is an anxiety attack waiting to happen.

We have created the pressure of frantic DOING…when what we really need is one big DOING-OVER.

When I think of what Jesus had been asked to accomplish in such a small window of time on earth, it is impossible to comprehend the kind of divine, critical thinking required to pull it off.

Attempted by anyone else, it would morph into an Emergency Room's worst nightmare…an understaffed, world-sized triage unit!

Here's what Jesus' "To Do List" looked like in Luke chapter 4.

First, Jesus dealt with the Devil's temptations for 40 days in the desert with no food and no rest. Then he traveled to Galilee, taught in their synagogues, was rejected at Nazareth, and driven out of town, skillfully avoiding being thrown off a cliff by the crowds. He traveled to Capernaum and taught in more synagogues, drove another demon out of yet another man, walked the long way to Simon's home, healed Simon's mother as well as a few more bystanders. Then he spoke to large, fickle crowds and healed the masses over and over with little to no break.

He was rightfully and righteously exhausted. And so on one morning at daybreak he went to a solitary place to pray and rest. Even there he could not find peace as the townspeople stalked him and tried to keep him there to heal more throngs of people and cast out even more demons. What pressure to be constantly doing the work of God!! And we think we just had a tough November.

He finally spoke up and explained that he needed to move on to other towns and continue to preach the good news of the kingdom "because that is why I was sent."

Right in those last 7 words, Jesus puts everything in perspective. He affirms that the most important task he had on earth was to preach the good news of eternal life.

He was saying he needed to stick to his purpose on earth. That sounds to me like the original Purpose Driven Manager with the biggest scope of all time.

He knew something we rarely think about. He knew there would always be those in need. He said so in Matthew 26:11, Mark 14:7. John 12:8, and way back in Deuteronomy 15:11. In Luke he ties these words to purpose and how that drives what we do each day.

Jesus triumphed because His work came from God, because He made time to pray for guidance, because he knew when to say "no", and because He kept His "yes" for the things that were important (Matthew 5:37). He targeted His actions with purpose, the purpose of a king. The King of Kings, to be exact.

Sometimes we need to quiet and remove ourselves from the crowd and the lists, find our focus and then cross off everything that doesn't make the A-List.

What of all the items on our lists will create a meaningful time with our families and friends?

Which of the tasks will provide a significant and sacred Christmas season for us and the people in our communities?

How can we give the gifts of time or the gifts of generous provision to those who would not have it otherwise?

Which items need to be crossed off?

Do we need 19 dishes on the Christmas table? Or do we need 19 Christmas memories around that table?

Only you and God know what He wants for you this Christmas. Take another look at those lists.

Prayer:

Jesus, take our hands and move them, take our minds and steer them, take our feet and send them where you want us to be. Remind us that when we seek you, we get our heads back on straight and our lists aligned with yours. We submit our paper and iCloud to you this Christmas.

"Take my life and let it be consecrated, Lord, to Thee.

Take my moments and my days, let them flow in ceaseless praise.

Take my love, my Lord, I pour at Thy feet its treasure store.

Take myself and I will be ever only, all for Thee."

(Lyrics by Frances Ridley Havergal)

Amen to that!

Follow Him ...Surrender All

Luke 5: 11; 17-20; 27-28
"So, they pulled their boats up on the shore, left everything and followed him." (v 11)

"One day as he was teaching, Pharisees and teachers of the law, who had come from every village of Galilee and from Judea and Jerusalem, were sitting there. And the power of the Lord was present for him to heal the sick. Some men came carrying a paralytic on a mat and tried to take him into the house to lay him before Jesus. When they could not find a way to do this because of the crowd, they went up on the roof and lowered him on his mat through the tiles into the middle of the crowd, right in front of Jesus.

When Jesus saw their faith, he said, "Friend, your sins are forgiven." (v 17-20)

After this, Jesus went out and saw a tax collector by the name of Levi sitting at his tax booth. "Follow me," Jesus said to him, and Levi got up, left everything, and followed him. (v 27-28)

Luke chapter 5 is a chapter of Faith in Action.

I came across an article whose title intrigued me: Give and Take: How the Rule of Reciprocation Binds Us, by Alix Spiegel. I read about a sociologist from Brigham Young University, Phillip Kunz, who conducted an experiment in 1974, sending 600 Christmas cards to strangers, whose names and addresses he found in directories for random towns. Cards trickled in until he had over 200, some with photos and long letters chronicling their lives. These were complete strangers. Why would they invest time and money to send cards to someone they did not know? It was the Rule of Reciprocation at work.

When someone gives you a gift, do you feel the need to give them a gift too? Maybe just to make it even and obtain the reciprocity that Kunz illustrated.

When the gift giver is the Almighty son of God, there is NO WAY in the world we can ever make it even with Him. What could we possibly give back to the God who has everything?

Now, what happens when He asks US to give everything, or rather give up everything and follow Him?

Can we give THAT gift? That's the million-dollar question of today's devotional.

It's a tall order to give everything. Admittedly, back in Jesus' time, some could not. But so many did. They were grateful to be healed. They were so moved by what they saw in the life and teaching of Jesus, the Christ, that all they could think of was to give ALL!

Sometimes we offer God our gifts of "good deeds". The effort by the men who lowered the paralytic onto the mat and down through the roof, so he could be healed by Jesus, represents incredible faith in action and one gigantic, good deed.

We may offer kindness to a stranger on Monday; attend bible study on Tuesday; work on a church committee on Wednesday; provide dinner for someone on Thursday; provide care for children or pets on Friday; spend time with a lonely friend on Saturday; attend and participate in church on Sunday.

These are all good things, good and vital gifts we can offer.

In addition to these kindnesses, there might be more he is asking of us...because there's that word: EVERYTHING.

What exactly is everything?

I'm reminded of an old hymn I love, "I Surrender All". The lyrics to the 1st verse & chorus are:

All to Jesus I surrender
All to Him I freely give.
I will ever love and trust Him
In His presence daily live.

I surrender all.
I surrender all.
All to Thee my blessed Savior
I surrender all.

But when I reflect on how I personally measure up to what is asked of us in this hymn, I think the chorus might be more accurately re-written like this:

I surrender some.
I surrender most.
Almost all to Thee my Savior
I surrender some.

And that changes everything!

I guess that's the point in Luke's Chapter 5.

Story after story you read words like: "and they left everything and followed him" ...everything!

Levi said, I will.

The man on the mat said I believe.

And his friends acted out their faith.

The people in these verses were committed to Jesus.

They believed they would be healed and they were. They believed in His Divinity.

Even when they didn't believe, Christ was faithful and He provided abundantly for their needs.

The same is true for us.

God Gave All to us, first the Garden of Eden, then the gifts of Mercy, Grace, Forgiveness, then the ultimate GIFT... His Son.

He gives every time we ask. Every time we knock, He opens a door! (Maybe not the door we wanted, but a door with our name on it.)

What would our "all" look like?

We give Him all of us. We surrender our lives to Him.

We leave everything behind, meaning in most cases we leave behind all our old ways, our old encumbrances, our old sins, and we move.

We move closer to Him through faith, through His Grace, His mercy, His forgiveness.

We move toward being more like Him. We move toward complete healing of our souls, a mighty revision of our hearts and remodeling of our minds, the thoughts we think, the words we say, the actions we take. Everything!

There are so many ways we can become more like Jesus.

It is never too late. We are never too old, too weak, too young, too much or too little!

He made us. He loves us freely, completely, incredibly selflessly. We will be transformed when we love Him back the same way.

We start by saying: I will follow Him! And along the way I will surrender all to Him.

All of my heart, my mind. All to Thee my blessed Savior, I surrender all!

Prayer:

Jesus, gentle Shepherd, we desire more of you. Give us the conviction to follow you wherever you may take us! Guide us to know what freely giving all to you means in our own individual lives. Free us to surrender all to you. Amen.

All We Need is Love!

Luke 6: 27-29

"But I tell you: Love your enemies, do good to those who hate you, bless those who curse you, pray for those who mistreat you. If someone strikes you on the cheek, turn to him the other also."

LOVE is the greatest source of power in the world. So why aren't we plugged in to that?

You would think by the number of songs written about love, that we would have a handle on how to "Put a little love in our hearts" by now. And if it's really true that "Love will keep us together", why are so many of us miles apart from each other?

We say, "All we need is love", but we are not even close to "A World Without Love".

And yet, long ago LOVE came down to the world to save us. Love came down in the form of Jesus Christ, and said some controversial things like: "Love those who hate you." That's the radical, wholly Jesus concept found in the New Testament.

And as much lip-service that we give to the altar of love, "loving those who hate you" is the polar opposite of what we are prone to do.

It is counterintuitive to our human nature. We can embrace love fully when it entails loving the easily loved and even that is hard at times. But God in His infinite wisdom knew it would take something monumental to get us to understand what love is, something that would shake us up. So, He sent Jesus to turn our thinking upside down in order to get us right side up again.

He was shaking the roots of our very core, pointing out where the first would be last and the last first, where LOVE would be the Law. "Truly He taught us to love one another. His law is love and His gospel is peace".

In 1957 Martin Luther King preached a sermon in the Dexter Avenue Baptist church, Montgomery, Alabama, on this very passage in Luke. In this sermon he said it was an "absolute necessity for the survival of our civilization" for us to love our enemies.

Martin Luther King said, "Love will save our world."

In his sermon he listed 3 things to help us with the practical part of "how do we do that"?

First, he said to take a hard look at ourselves. Or paraphrasing the words of Jesus, first take a look in the mirror and remove the large "beam in our own eye" before we get all self-righteous about the "mote in our brother's eye".

Second, he says to find the GOOD in the other person. No matter how impossible this might be, find something good.

Paul speaks about the convoluted, complex nature of men in Romans 7:19 "For what I do is not the good I want to do; No, the evil I do not want to do—this I keep on doing."

I think Paul understands us well. We mean well, but we mess up. If we want the grace of understanding for our own struggle with good and evil, then we must give it to others, both those who love us and those who hate us.

3) Third and maybe hardest of all is this one. When the opportunity comes one day for us to defeat our enemies, (with the exception of Satan), we are to resist the temptation to defeat them. Why? Because when Jesus tells us to love our enemies, that does not in any way include trampling over them when they are down, or taunting them with "I told you so" comments, or otherwise playing "God" in the situation, exacting judgment on that person.

In the end we don't have to LIKE that person or what they do or say, or become best buds with them. However, Jesus does command us to LOVE them. He tells us not to trample on them when we get the opportunity but to offer a hand when they are down. He says to get over ourselves and turn the other cheek!

I think we are given an inordinate number of opportunities to do just that in our lives. But we may not have recognized them for what they are: examples of Jesus calling out to us to "do the right thing". LOVE!

"Darkness cannot drive out darkness; only LIGHT can do that. Hate cannot drive out hatred; only LOVE can do that." Martin Luther King

"Above all, love each other deeply." 1 Peter 4:8

"My command is this: LOVE each other as I have loved you." John 15:12

Prayer:

Jesus, you gave us this command to love, no matter what and no matter who. You know that hating others poisons us. Empower us to take the bold step of loving our enemies. Teach us to love completely and without fail, just like you showed us long ago.

Amen.

Beyond a Shadow of a Doubt

Luke 7: 7-10

"But say the word, and my servant will be healed.

When Jesus heard this, he was amazed at him, and turning to the crowd following him, he said, I tell you; I have not found such great faith even in Israel.

Then the men who had been sent returned to the house and found the servant well."

Faith. Rock, solid faith. That's what this man had. He was a centurion, a man not unlike our military, who lived by the chain of command. He recognized clearly that Jesus was at the head of this chain of command. He knew Jesus had the power to heal his servant. He didn't need Jesus to appear at his doorstep to prove that. He didn't need Jesus to have a blinking neon sign attached to his entourage, saying "This is the LORD!" "Have Faith!"

He didn't even need the Star of Bethlehem to direct him.

He knew! He believed! That's the picture Luke paints of this centurion. He didn't let doubt get in the middle of his belief.

Faith moves mountains. Doubt just stews and never gets past inertia.

The story of the centurion ends well. Faith shown. Prayer answered.

But here we are and bad things happen. We need Jesus. And he isn't walking on our streets, or even at a Convention Center across the country.

He isn't in a boat on a lake near us. He isn't in one or our deserts praying.

Well, He IS all these places, we just don't always recognize that.

He tells us to call on him and He will answer.

And we wonder if our problem is too big or too small for His time. The God of the Universe is just as interested in our details as He is in our big picture.

And yet bad things still happen to good people, even people of great faith.

I don't pretend to know why. Neither will I join those who minimize losses, offer a prescriptive formula for why some prayers are answered and others are not, equate your assets to the amount of faith you have, or pronounce judgment on those whose prayers were not answered in the desirable way.

What I can say is the battle between good and evil is still being fought. And evil wins quite a few of those battles. But I know that through every battle I fight, I am not alone.

As much as I love answers and solutions, I have learned the best offering I can give to others is to withhold my solution and to just show up. Listen. Sometimes use words.

And so, I believe.

Without a shadow of a doubt, I know He will show up for me. He will walk with me through my loss, hold me through a 9-hour vertigo attack on a cold basement floor, carry me through failure, and stay with me through fear.

When everything is gone, He is still there.

I know that in all the worst times there is a space, so sweet, so sacred where I feel His presence. In the trial and in the tragedy, He is there.

"The Lord is near to all who call on him." (Psalm 145:18)

Prayer:

Lord, thank you for the example of this man's faith. Thank you for your faithfulness to us.

We long to have faith like the Centurion.

We believe that when we ask, you will answer.

We know when your words are upon our lips and rest within our minds and hearts, you are delighted by that.

We ask for unshakeable, undeniable faith!

We ask for sacred moments, knowing you are there.

Amen.

From Darkness to Light

"The man from whom the demons had gone out begged to go with him (Jesus), but Jesus sent him away, saying, "Return home and tell how much God has done for you."

"So, the man went away and told all over town how much Jesus had done for him." Luke 8: 38-39

This is a story of a man with no hope.

No hope means living with no anticipation of what might happen next, just a dreary, depressing state of mind that makes 24 hours feel like eternity.

No hope looks like utter despair. No hope is darkness.

It is the very opposite of John the Baptist's anticipatory words paraphrased:

"Be ready, for there's something coming…something wonderful coming!"

Now, we'll begin again.

This is the story of a man with no hope, a man who had lived in darkness for many years and one day met the Son of God and had his life turned upside down.

The encounter begins like this: It had been a long, dark and stormy night.

It was right after Jesus and the disciples had experienced the raging storm at sea, where Jesus quieted the waves and the wind. (Luke 8: 24-25) Finally, they arrived on the other side of the lake at a place called Gerasenes.

As soon as Jesus stepped off the boat and onto the shore he was met by a wild man, out of his mind, naked and possessed by multiple demons. (One source said there were over 2,000 demons living in his body and mind).

This man was so afflicted by Satan's demonic beings, that he had to be chained hand and foot. He would break away from the chains in such a rage that he caused fear among all the people of the town and had to hide away in the tombs. Other false prophets had tried to exorcise the demons out of this man to no avail. His life was stuck in a quagmire of living hell. His days were made up of endless torture.

"When he saw Jesus, he cried out and fell at his feet, shouting at the top of his voice, 'What do you want with me, Jesus, Son of the Most High God?'" (Luke 8:28)

Jesus asked the name of the demons and the demons responded "Legion", because there were so many residing in this man's body.

So, Jesus commanded all the demons out of the man and the demons entered the bodies of nearby pigs. The pigs were so possessed that they rushed down a steep bank into the lake and were drowned.

After watching this spectacle, the people came back to see the former wild man returned to sanity, dressed, and sitting beside Jesus, having an actual conversation with him.

Light had finally come to this man's life, but ironically, this made the townsfolk so afraid that they told Jesus to leave their town quickly. They were a lot like us. They didn't like change.

As Jesus was leaving, the man asked Jesus if he could follow him.

But Jesus sent him away and told him to go back to his town and "tell everyone what God had done for him that day". The man who had been possessed by demons did just that, and in so doing became one of the earliest evangelists in the time of Jesus. Jesus turned darkness into light for this man.

Jesus wanted this man to plant seeds for the kingdom. What better restoration of a soul that had lived in darkness for so much of his life, than to allow him to be a planter of seeds from the Light?

Jesus causes many of us to come full circle in our lives. We are given second chances through his healing.

When we ask of him, "What do you want with me, Jesus?", we open ourselves to the miracle of change.

I can look to Jesus with great hope and great anticipation that I too can be changed. I can hold on to the hope that I can have a second chance at goodness; a second opportunity to be merciful; another chance to be the person he planned for me to be all along.

I don't have to live as if the chains were still holding me back. I don't have to think that because I am not where I wanted to be by now, that it's over.

It is NEVER over with Jesus. He can change my darkness into light at any moment. He is the giver of miracles, the healer of our bodies and souls. He is the Light!

To be touched by God means to be forever changed by Him. And the gift of hope and change can live in us as long as we have breath.

Prayer:

Jesus, Deliverer of our sins, giver of hope and light,

Thank you for loving and looking at me through the eyes of a merciful Father.

Drive out despair and change my heart forever.

Amen.

Listen to Me

Luke 12: 22-34. (The Passion Translation)

"Listen to me. Never let worry enter your hearts. Never worry about any of your needs, such as food or clothing. For your life is infinitely more than just food or the clothing you wear."

"Does worry add anything to your life? Can it add one more year, or even one day?"

"Your heavenly Father knows your every need and will take care of you."

Practical advice about worry, found in the gospel of Luke.

Oh, what peace that would be...to never worry, never have an uncertain moment.

There is not a one among us who has not been filled with anxious thought. None who has completely mastered the art of a "worry-free" life. So, let's pay close attention.

In the Bible when scripture is led with an imperative statement or words are repeated, this is God telling us to pay attention. Those flashing imperative neon lights also imply command. Jesus is issuing a command, not a suggestion, in the topics of worry, apprehension, and peace.

Notice how Jesus begins that passage with the words "Listen to me."

I imagine Jesus leaning forward with emphasis, maybe even lowering his voice, causing the disciples to draw closer in order to hear his next words.

Think of the times when you began a sentence with "Listen to me!" They aren't words you use in just any conversation. What follows is usually something of significance, or critical to the moment as well as the listener.

Those words are used by parents all over the world, by fervent friends, by couples. And if you are the person being told to "listen", it is best to have "ears that hear", if you know what I mean.

Right after the "listen to me" sentence, Jesus says "Never let worry enter your hearts."

The lead word is "Never" and "never" is a tall order. He is using this word to emphasize the focus needed to battle doubt and dread.

I think He is saying that worry is so powerful and so easily multiplied once we let it into our hearts, that it disrupts any peace we may have had in the first place.

Personally, I view worry as a sneaky mental troublemaker. It enters with a tiny thought of the smallest possibility of something going wrong and quickly expands to a prophecy of disastrous doom and gloom. From possibility to prophecy in a minute and a half! That's how worry works!

Like doubt, its 3rd cousin, worry is crippling. It is the paralyzing force in all good plans, robbing us of our momentum, our progression to the positive, and our peace.

For example, have you ever seen the movie, The Intern? Great cast: Anne Hathaway, Robert De Niro, Adam DeVine… all powerful actors. That movie is about the war between constant agitation and peace. It is also about the power of combining the strengths of age and wisdom with the strengths of youth and innovation.

If you watch this movie, you will see the progression in Anne Hathaway's character from a successful, production driven, angst ridden life, to a purposeful life of significance, managed by inner peace. It is intriguing to watch that transformation. In the end she is able to continue being her innovative self only by managing her doubts through peace. The inner peace she attains then allows her to relate more closely to those around her. Consequently, she projects empathy to the world, her family at home and her family at work. Peace becomes a gift she gives to those in her circle.

When we kick worry out of our lives and project a calm presence, there is an additional benefit of becoming the kind of people others are drawn to. Peace is a powerful magnet.

Jesus wants us to give up the worry game not only to give us the peace He knows we need, but also to use us to draw others closer to Him.

Inner peace to outer peace. Jesus is promoting that kind of peace. He IS that kind of peace, the Prince of Peace and His circle is the world, including us.

"Peace be unto you" of olden days is equivalent to our present-day "Have a good day". They both are hopeful blessings we offer to each other as we enter and leave their presence. The older version seems wiser to me. It is offering a way to have that good day through peace.

Luke's friend, Paul, in Romans 12:18, goes even further and says: "If it is possible, as far as it depends on you, live at peace with everyone."

Be at peace with yourself and in so doing, it will be much easier to be at peace with others.

Jesus also says in John 14:27 "Peace I leave with you; my peace I give you. I do not give to you as the world gives. Do not let your hearts be troubled and do not be afraid."

That's a promise and a gift all rolled into one, given by the Prince of Peace.

Prayer:

Father, we need you. We are filled with worry, grief, and apprehension. We are troubled to the point of losing sleep and losing ourselves. The world is "too much with us" and we can't seem to let go. We want to breathe easily once again, to walk in harmony with you. Help us listen carefully in the private time of earnest prayer; in time spent reading your Word.

And when you say, "Listen to me", give us "ears to hear" as you speak to our hearts. Amen.

And Who is My Neighbor?

Luke 10: 29 "But he wanted to justify himself, so he asked Jesus, "And who is my neighbor?"

Luke records an incident where an expert of the law asked Jesus the question of what he must do to inherit eternal life. Jesus asks him what was written in the law, and the law expert answered, 'Love the Lord your God with all your heart and all your soul; with all your strength and with all your mind' and 'Love your neighbor as yourself'. Jesus replied, "You have answered correctly. Do this and you will live." But the expert in law wanted to justify himself so he asked Jesus a follow up question. It was "And who is my neighbor?"

So, taking it to the next level, Jesus turns the question back to the expert and tells the story of the Good Samaritan. Jesus asks in verse 36, "Who of the three, do you think was a neighbor to the man who fell into the hands of the robbers?" The expert in the law responds, "The one who had mercy on him." Jesus then told him, "Go and do likewise."

It is imminently clear how God feels about neighbors in Leviticus 19:18, "Do not seek revenge or bear a grudge against anyone but love your neighbor as yourself." And in Mark 12:31 we are taught that the second greatest commandment is: "You shall love your neighbor as yourself."

This is the recipe for how Jesus wants us to live in the world.

Christ's message embraced the whole of creation. Lutheran, Paul Santmire wrote in the mid-1990's, "The Captain of our salvation, Jesus Christ, cares for the ark of this universe and its eternal destiny. He cares for every creature on board, and in turn calls upon the human passengers of this universal vessel to care likewise for the whole vessel and all its creatures."

So, to Jesus-following Christians our whole world is filled with neighbors to be loved. We are justified by grace alone but that gives us freedom to choose wisely, through Jesus' examples in Luke and throughout the New Testament.

God knows that in being the good neighbor, we become more like Christ, loving selflessly, all who enter our sphere of influence.

When we view our neighbor as anyone God places in our lives, then our influence widens. And by "neighbor" I'm referencing anyone with whom we have communication throughout our days. Face to face, phone, social media, work, school, church, our homes, on and on, those are the personal and global circles. Thinking about this wider scope of "neighbors" means thinking outside of our usual boxes.

Elbert Hubbard (an American writer, artist and philosopher) said: "Your neighbor is the man who needs you."

My favorite quote on neighbors, however, is from Fred Rogers, the Presbyterian minister who designed and appeared in Mr. Roger's Neighborhood. It is the line in his song, "Won't you be my neighbor?" This one implies reaching out to others to actually search for your life's neighbors.

It highlights the idea of inclusiveness that we know Jesus would embrace. The very act of asking is placing the other person's needs ahead of ours, or at least on a par with ours. It is the "love our neighbors as ourselves" part of Jesus's commandment.

When we do all this, our lives are enriched, our good seeds have a fertile ground in which to grow. We show love, kindness, mercy.

We then are living Jesus' definition of a good neighbor and that is a purpose greater than ourselves. We become "the one who shows mercy."

Prayer:

Jesus,

Help us to know that you have placed us where you want us for now; that you have designed who our neighbors are and will be and that you have a purpose for that arrangement.

Help us to remember that our "neighbors" reach beyond our own roads, streets, communities, and countries.

Guide us to honor your words in Luke 10…that a neighbor is "the one who has mercy."

Amen.

This Little Light of Mine

"No one lights a lamp and puts it in a place where it will be hidden, or under a bowl. Instead, he puts it on its stand, so that those who come in may see the light."

Luke 11: 33.

I used to read this scripture verse and wonder why it would just state the obvious. What was the point?

Of course you are not going to light a lamp and then hide it! Who does that?

It turns out that we all "hide our light under a bushel", in one way or another.

The reasons we do this are as diverse as our population.

One reason could be we don't think we are really needed. We think someone else would be better at whatever it is. And since someone has been doing that task for some time, there is no need for our help. As to this last one, I would offer this thought: maybe that person is always doing it because no one has stepped up. And to the person "always" doing that job, I would offer that sometimes when we finally step away, there is someone ready and waiting to step in.

Another reason we might hide our light has to do with the feeling of self-doubt. That feeling robs us of so many opportunities and moments to share Jesus' good news.

Until I started looking at Luke 11:33 from a different angle, I didn't think it applied to me or ever would. And of course, I was 100% wrong. I just hadn't hit that roadblock yet, the one labeled self-doubt.

No one comes out of this life unscathed by self-doubt, no one. You can move through life working hard, making friends, having good relationships with your fellow man, living in an aura of confidence. And then one day, something in your life starts to shift a bit, just a little bit. Maybe it's a word whispered that you weren't meant to hear; maybe it was a just a feeling that you didn't fit in, or what you had to say wasn't important; a feeling of being invisible. Or maybe you had unfounded insecurities for one reason or another.

Perhaps you were dealt a huge set back that hit you squarely in the forehead and adjusted your self-image accordingly. And in the process of righting that image, you lost your light, or hid it for safe keeping.

One thing is for certain when self-doubt enters your life, you eventually lose your inner motivation, the part of you that keeps you balanced and upright; the part of you that lets you walk into a room, holding your head up and not be intimidated.

You begin to hang out on the periphery of the room, participating a whole lot less, and pretty much silencing your conversation or comments out of fear they would not land well on the ears of others around you. You feel "less than". So, you hide your light. And you decrease or stop entirely your participation in life outside of your own world. You become part of what you once were.

Your light dims or extinguishes completely.

If any of this rings true for you, it might be time to reassess. The problem may be that you need to shine your light in a different "room", with different people surrounding you. Or the problem might be that you have hidden your light under a bowl of your own making.

Jesus does not want us to hide our light, our unique personalities, or our gifts. He wants us to use our gifts. What good does hiding our gifts do for the world or His cause?

If you need healing to get to point of relighting your lamp, please seek guidance.

Good counselors are Lights unto themselves. Good friends are priceless.

If you need encouragement, He has provided that in the form of His wonderful Word and the people He has placed in your life. The people who want to help are the ones whose opinions count.

If you want to hear from the Lord, draw near to him in prayer. Ask, seek, find his answers in unceasing prayer. Seek the timeless gift of His Word!

If you need direction or re-direction, as it was in my case, see Luke 11:33. One day I "happened" upon these verses for the hundredth time. This time I was ready to hear the words for my own edification. He directed me to His guidance. I read the words, "No one lights a lamp and puts it in a place where it will be hidden". I stopped right there with the biggest lump in my throat, tears down my face and finally conviction in my heart. I knew I had to get back out there and put one foot in front of the other, step by step, re-enter the world of shining my light, little by little. I hear my sister, Lettie, telling me, "Poco a poco se va lejos" Little by little, one goes far", and I am renewed once again. You never know how much good you can cause by sharing your words with someone else.

I encourage you now to: Find the right room, find the right people. And most importantly, find your light.

Shine it as brightly as you can. There is someone who needs your particular gift right now. They are waiting with anticipation for an answer to their prayers.

Your light may be their answer!

It's Christmas season and we are confronted with the brightest Light in the sky, the Star of Bethlehem! The Light that guided the Wise men to Christ.

No clouds were in the way that night. The setting was perfect. But the Wise Men had to look up, right? They had to seek the Light in order to follow the Light, and then one day be the light.

Prayer:

Light of the World,

Thank you for illuminating our way! Thank you for telling us that we have what it takes to be a light in our world. Thank you for reminding us that we are enough, worthy enough to shine.

Thank you for reminding us to look up in order to find your light!

Amen.

O Holy Night! Joy to the World, the Lord has come! Let earth receive her King!

Luke 2:8-14

"And there were shepherds abiding in the fields nearby, keeping watch over their flocks by night. An angel of the Lord appeared to them, and the glory of the Lord shone around them, and they were terrified. But the angel said to them, "Do not be afraid. I bring you good news of great joy that will be for all people. Today in the town of David, a Savior has been born to you; he is Christ, the Lord. This will be a sign to you: You will find a baby wrapped in cloths and lying in a manger."

Suddenly a great company of the heavenly host appeared with the angel, praising God and saying, "Glory to God, in the highest, and on earth peace to men."

All through the Christmas season, we sit by the fire, counting on being lifted up by the miracles we have seen year after year in our favorite Christmas movies. American movie culture paints a broad brush of hope with its iconic movies of Christmas: the 1947 movie, "Miracle on 34th Street" with Edmund Gwenn, Mareen O'Hara, David Payne and Natalie Wood, "The Bishop's Wife" (also 1947) with Cary Grant, Lorretta Young and David Niven, and of course Jimmy Stewart, Donna Reed, and Lionel Barrymore in "It's a Wonderful Life" (1946).

We are drawn to miracles because we see their magic, and begin to draw one with our name on it, while our spirits rise.

The night before Christmas, long ago, held a miracle for certain shepherds: a supernatural intervention, a long and fearful journey through dangerous lands, the hunt for a newborn, and one extravagant promise. How could they find him with only the name of the city given to them? This is the movie we long to watch, the one with the miraculous ending.

The night before Christmas still holds the same magic it did for me many decades ago.

The anticipation comes for a different reason now. The wonder is from a different place. But the joy in my heart feels the same, just better, deeper.

Christmas Eve Candlelight service is a mystical, sacred tradition. Walking into the church, I see all its candles ready and waiting to come alive. The music that stirs my soul and the loved ones by my side, create in me a gratitude that overflows from my soul and my eyes. I am undone by the soprano voice, singing "Fall on your knees! Oh, hear the angel voices. Oh, night divine. Oh, night when Christ was born!"

It's a night of promise, a night of great anticipation and hope!

The miracle of the babe in the manger foreshadows the hope we feel about good overcoming evil, and the rise of our own soul's worth, the hunt for our place in the world.

Like the shepherds, we travel a journey searching for a miracle, casting our hope on sometimes good, sometimes fruitless things. We spend years finding, losing, and finding Him again.

We get a chance for a new beginning every time we fall on our knees and let Him in.

That's what Jesus is to us...a new beginning. He is our miracle. And the movie is our life.

"No more let sin and sorrow grow, nor thorns infest the ground. He comes to make His blessings flow, far as the curse is found!"

The Joy from Jesus, given to us by God, followed by the gift of the Holy Spirit, the miracle of a lifetime partner, the Holy Trinity in all its glory. What better hope than this, what better miracle!

"O Holy Night, let every heart prepare Him room!"

Prayer:

Father, we don't have to look far to find you. Your hope is not hidden from us. You have written our names on the miracles of your gifts.

We bow before the manger and rise with you to receive the wonders of your love.

Joy to the World!

Amen!

Always Ever Preparing the Way

From the very beginning of time when God was about to form the world, the Holy Spirit was hovering over the waters, creating energy and promise, preparing the world for what was yet to come.

I can get caught up in that picture. Nothing but vast, empty space. God present, ready to utter the Creation Words, the Word present in Jesus Christ, and the Holy Spirit present, ready to do the work of transformation. All of space would be transformed into our universe by the Almighty Trinity. God, Jesus, the Holy Spirit, all present at the beginning.

What a holy visual!

Read it with me for the thousandth time and see it anew THIS time:

Genesis 1: 1-2

"In the beginning God created the heavens and the earth. Now the earth was formless and empty, darkness was over the surface of the deep, and the Spirit of God was hovering over the waters."

Genesis 1:1-2 pacts so much HOLY into those 2 verses, that it takes me a long time to get past them. I like to linger over the words, picturing the power in the empty space that was to become something miraculous, something holy.

I used to rush through the entire Creation passages in chapters 1 and 2 with a sort of casual acknowledgement that the Bible had to start "somewhere" but since I already knew that story, I wanted to get on to something new.

I was unaware, didn't know that no words were wasted words in the bible, that every story was chosen for a purpose.

Let's draw close and focus on God's miraculous gift of preparing us for everything in our lives.

He was at work in me even then. I needed to recognize what I didn't know in order to recognize the truth when I read it. He was preparing me to become a close and careful reader of the Word, and eventually to be able to uncover meaning behind the passages to come.

He is a patient teacher and He loved me through every possible stage of growth. He loves me still, teaching me more every day when I open my heart to Him asking the Holy Spirit, living in me, to guide my days.

I wonder how He has prepared you today? How has He loved you throughout your life? How can we ever thank Him enough?

He wants our sincere gratitude, our loving acknowledgement of His presence in our lives, and our joy and gladness for what He has done for us. And He wants our commitment to use those gifts for good in the world. He is in the business of ever, always preparing the way for us.

Prayer:

Lord, teach us to listen, learn, and serve with grateful, knowing hearts. Amen.

Hope is the Thing

Lately my thoughts have been going back, way back to my childhood. It could be all the Hallmark Christmas movies I have been watching, or just the increased time in solitude, where my own thoughts and memories come flooding back to me in overwhelmingly real segments.

(LOOKING UP)

A lot of those segments include times looking at my church, walking to my church, being inside my church surrounded by stained glass windows on all sides, singing in my church and hearing the stories of God, Jesus, and the Holy Spirit.

It was such a big part of our lives and I'm so thankful for that.

I can still see clearly the little church I grew up in, just across the street, a hearty stone's throw away. It didn't feel little then, it felt massive. It was built on a small knoll, such that its basement was on the ground floor and its main sanctuary was a staircase upwards. For that reason, the steeple was high enough that everyone had to look way, way up to see it.

Bells rang joyfully from the bell tower and if you stood on the outside stairway your whole body could feel the reverberation of those bells.

It was a great place to be on Christmas Eve! The last service was the Midnight Candlelight service. The soft reflection of the light from those hundred candles, and the magic of the voices singing the 200-year-old lyrics of Silent Night, Holy Night, was seared into your soul for life. Nothing was more sacred. Nothing was better than hearing my family sing in

3-part harmony as we stood with tears in our eyes during all six verses. Nothing was more sacred.

(LOOKING OUT)

All were welcome in our church. All were welcome at the table of communion, at the altar of conviction, and in the prayers of the people. If you walked through the door of our church, you were greeted with smiles and people moving closer in their pew to make room. If you came back, you were looked out for and called by name.

Every window was made of stained glass, renditions of some part of the New Testament. I was mesmerized by those windows. And I loved thinking about the stories they told, stories of the Son, illuminated by the light of the sun, coming through those beautiful windows.

(LOOKING FROM WITHIN)

My head was full of bible stories because of the pillars of that church, and I am not talking about brick and mortar. One of those pillars was Miss Dorothy Drummond, a tiny, stooped, elderly Sunday school teacher. Miss Drummond told us, in great detail, all the stories of the Bible. And she had the biggest book full of colorful pages and stories of long ago.

I grew up thinking the Bible was one gigantic story book of tales of courageous, hopeful people of God. I felt their stories take life when she told them to us and we read from the picture filled, oversized book she brought to our class. I loved the names of the teenagers, Shadrach, Meshach and Abednego, loved how those names rolled off your tongue when you said them out loud and of course the story of their oversized faith. I wanted to be brave like those teenagers.

When we read about Daniel in the Lion's den, I pictured Daniel with faith as big as the mountain we were supposed to be able to faithfully fling into the sea. I wanted to have faith like Daniel.

I imagined David first as the peaceful shepherd boy in the fields writing his poetry and then as a warrior for God, and finally as a father himself. He was my favorite then and I wanted to write poetry like his and lead people to God through my words.

I loved when it was my turn to hold the book. The pages came alive then because they were right in front of your face.

The hope of the past, infused in our present lives, giving us solid faith and hope for the future, that's what my church gave me as a child. And if ever there were a convicting statement about the importance of the body of Christ reaching out inclusively with open doors, that was it for me.

Hope is the thing that grounds us from wherever our beginnings were to our places now. Sometimes we have to look back in wonder in order to see the joy ahead.

Prayer:

Holy Father, create in us the desire to learn more about you. You designed us for connection. Help us to love so deeply that we are always looking for ways to bring others into the reach of your love. Remind us that it is by looking up and within, that we are able to look out for those around us. Amen.

This devotion is dedicated to my childhood church and hometown of Clarksburg, West Virginia where my family and neighbors were securely tucked into the terraced streets of Adamston. You were the foundation of my faith.

See, I am Doing a New Thing!

For anyone who longs for yet another chance to start over; for a complete re-do of a time, place, word, or action, the book of Isaiah is full of ideas.

Isaiah 12:3

"See, I am doing a new thing. Now it springs up; do you not perceive it? I am making a way in the wilderness and streams in the wasteland."

New Year's Eve is not my favorite holiday. What I l do look forward to is a good meal at 4:00 o'clock with friends and then home by 7:00, in my PJ's, curled up with a good book. The next day is the start of a brand-new year and for me an informal, personal inventory of the "state of my heart". I don't believe in wallowing in the mistakes of the past. That has never served me well. But what does make sense to me is time set aside for figuring out what I want to do to become a better person. The question I ask myself is: What do I want more of in my life?

Isaiah 12:3 would have me frame it like this: What new outlook or addition to my life will place me on a path toward a new and improved human being?

Last year I decided I needed to work harder not to judge other's preferences that were different from mine. I don't care if you like your crust made with cauliflower bits or full out glutenous flour. I can make either one. I don't care if you like a live tree or an artificial one. They're both beautiful. I don't even care if you are a dog person or a cat person. What I do care about are the bigger issues in life. But I found I had started to react openly in a judgmental way, from the expression on my face, to the words I chose, I took a long look at myself and decided that I needed to change. I could still feel passionately about the topic de jour, but my goal would be to listen carefully to the other person, hear them out, stop trying to plan the words I would say when it was my turn in the conversation. When I did that, I found that my response was more often a kinder, more loving version. I began to look more for what we had in common than what I wanted to say to persuade the other guy to my way of thinking.

The result was better connection in every conversation, more genuinely open, inclusive communication. I was building a way through the wilderness and wasteland of division. I still had my opinions, my personal take on life. But the things we had in common were more important to me than what we didn't. My personal end result was that I felt more peace, more love, and more hope.

This is the place we build on, the point from which we move forward together in conversation, in our communities, and in our country. I can't affect the world, but I can affect something in my own world.

You may have things you want to reflect on too.

Whatever your introspection leads you to do, or re-do, know that the One who guided you to that place, will help you through it. He will show you the way and He will make that way better.

He will even carve out a path in a complete wasteland of ruin if that's the case.

If ever there were a time to become a better human being, it is now. It will always be now.

Happy New Year to you! Happy new YOU to the world!

Prayer:

Lord, you make all things new. You see the best in us and urge us to find it ourselves.

Change our hearts, Lord. Help us to see the best in each other as we hold on to hope in this changing world. Amen.

Part Six:

What We Learn from Prayer

The mark of an extraordinary relationship is when that's the first person you want to call when something happens. The words flow easily and nothing is withheld. Or there are no words and you sit in the comfort of compatible silence. Our Creator desires a relationship just like that with us. He wants to be number ONE on our speed dial day or night.

Prayer is conversation we have with God that draws us closer to Him.

He doesn't care when, where, or how we pray. Prayer can be in the silence of the forest, or an early morning sunrise. It can happen in the shelter of a favorite chair or the discomfort of a middle seat in a 10-hour flight.

Sometimes the words flow in abundance from our hearts and sometimes we can't find a single word to say.

I offer a few prayers in this chapter for those moments when we struggle to find words of our own.

Prayers for All Times!

How sweet is the feeling of newly answered prayer. How deep is our gratitude.

1) A Prayer to start your day:

Dear Lord,

I invite You into my day, into every part of it, the people I will interact with, the circumstances that await me, the words I say, and the thoughts I have.

Be present with me, Lord. Quiet me so that I may focus on what is important at this minute.

Heal me so that I may be a healing balm to others.

Give me your abundant love so I may show it abundantly to others.

Infuse in me your grace so that I may offer graciousness throughout my day.

Let everything I do reflect my gratitude for all you are to me today and all my tomorrows.

Amen.

2) A Prayer for Any Time

Lord, what do you want me to learn today? How can I give from the abundance in my life to those who have so little.

I ask for more generosity, more acceptance, more kindness, and more love. I ask for all of these for my daily needs and for the needs of others.

I ask that I might listen carefully and clearly to those around me so that I can understand their needs. And then I ask for wisdom to act in the way that works the best.

Most of all I want your love reflected in my life today!

Amen.

3) A Prayer in the Midst of Our Brokenness

Lord, the world is just too much right now. We are in need of so many things.

We cry out to you in the dark of the night and all through the endless day.

We call for your mercy. We ask for healing.

We need your understanding as we move through difficult times.

We cry out for what and who we have lost, for the people we long to be with.

We yearn for the "normal' that once defined our lives.

Our losses are too many to manage without you.

We are brokenhearted and we need you to hold us close.

Deliver us from the things of the world that crush us.

Watch over us.

Amen.

4) Prayer for loved ones who are gravely ill

God, we need a miracle. None seem readily available. None of the diagnoses or prognoses are good.

But we worship a God who parts the sea and moves the mountains, so we put this in your hands. We are asking that you change the outcome in ways that only You can do.

Be with those who love and care for the sick. Be with them as they manage difficult situations.

We pray for the words to say, the questions to ask.

We ask that you remove anxiety so our loved ones can walk through this valley with calm in the face of very little cause for hope. Lord, be hope to them.

Come into this complicated mess and bring healing.

Amen.

5) Prayer for those who offer care.

We are asking blessings of safety, guidance, and wisdom for those who do your work on earth.

We are thankful for a heritage of kindness and generosity passed on for generations to come.

Amen.

6) Prayer for when you don't feel like you fit.

Lord, help me when I feel dismissed, disillusioned, disappointed.

Remind me of the times I have fallen short on those same things.

Assure me that you are my greatest friend, my best guide and counselor.

Transform my heart!

Redo my thoughts!
Renew my grace.
Let it be so.

7) Prayer for when you are overcome with fear.

Oh, Lord, I can't catch my breath. It's well past midnight and my heart feels out of control, pulse racing. Keep me safe.

I tell myself You are in control, not the world.

I tell myself my body will right itself in time.

But still the pressure in my chest is tightening.

The noise in my ears is disconcerting and dissonant.

I feel vulnerable and afraid. I'm 30 seconds away from calling 9-1-1.

I slow my breathing...in and out...slowly 1...2...3, and calm returns and I exhale thoughts of thankfulness. I asked. You answered.

I feel my chest relax and my mind unwind.

Thank you for your presence and your peace throughout this ordeal.

Thank you for walking with me through this valley, Lord.

Amen.

8) Prayers for when you don't know what to do with your life

Lord, I feel clueless in my own life.
I am lost and without direction.
I don't know the answers to any of the important questions and I feel like a clock is ticking on this final exam.
I have no spread sheet of numbers to help me analyze my life or its goals.
I have no data from needs assessments, no summary from any poll.

I've lost confidence to know what is best for me.
I can't find my inner compass.
And I have lost trust in others.

I need you to lead me, to show me who to trust and whose words to set aside.
Hear my words, Lord.
Come to my side.
Show me the way, again.
Amen.

9) A Prayer when there is no peace

Lord, there is strife in my life.
There is tension in my world and in my heart.

There is no peace in my soul right now.

The subtle sarcasm, the nuanced snark, all mess with my head and my trust.

It goes on and on and I don't know why.

Where is this tension coming from?
Is it me? Is it something I have done or said?
Some look I have given or not given?

How do I fix what I do not understand?
There is strife in my life and it isn't good.

Keep me from the useless, destructive act of revenge or the act of blame.

Point me to peace, Lord.
Clear my head and clean out my heart so I can move forward.
Bring me clarity, Lord, or bring me peace.
Amen.

10) A Prayer for patience

Lord, I want to know the answer.
I have prayed about this for years and I am tired of waiting.
I'm frustrated and I feel myself sinking into sadness.
Lord, remind me that my thoughts are not your thoughts.
Even though I can't see the solution, let me be assured that everything holds together when you are at the center. No matter what else falls away, you will remain.
Help me to believe.
Amen.

11) A Prayer for babies and their families

Father, we know just how much you love your children.
I am praying that you have gone ahead and know where the path leads.
We trust you with the in-between of life...where things are right now and where you want them to be.
We are praying for strength, stamina, and joy.
Joy in the moment...joy in knowing the blessing you have given is growing and becoming whole with every breath. Bless this baby as he comes into the world.
Bless the life.
Bless the one who carries that life and bless the father.
Bless all those who will be in this child's life. Place them where you want them to be as this child grows.

As we wait, give us patience. As we celebrate this life, we rejoice in the blessings you have already given.
Amen.

12) A Prayer for Mercy

Heavenly Father,
You are our Healer!
You have given us every mercy; every second chance and we are grateful.
We are putting this disease completely into Your Hands and asking for a miracle.
Heal your child, Lord.
Part the seas again and give him rescue on safe ground.
Ground your child, so he can stand up under pressure and turmoil.
Be with her. Hold her hand. Steady her and calm the seas of her emotions.
Bring every good thing to work in this healing.
We thank you for all you will have done and for all you are doing.
Thank you for the peace you have offered.
Come, Lord Jesus!

13) Praying with the person who needs healing

I pray that your broken body will respond to the mighty Hand of God and heal completely.
I pray that your medical team will have clear insights into all that matters.
I pray that during all of this, those around you will surround you with uplifting words, acts of love, and fervent prayers.
I pray that those you love will be comforted as you are

comforted by His grace.
I pray that you will be whole again.
Amen.

14) A Prayer for courage

I pray that you have the courage to stand up for yourself, for your needs and your desires.

I pray that you don't let your own needs get buried beneath the cries of those around you.

I pray for continued wisdom to know the right thing to do.

15) Prayer for when we struggle with big decisions:

Lord, we are struggling with decisions too big for us right now.
We are in the middle of mayhem and need to be centered.
All around, things are crumbling and we have nothing to hold on to.
And yet you have said hold on to you.
You have said, "Come to me, all you who are weary and burdened, and I will give you rest."
You have said, "Take my yoke upon you and learn from me, for I am gentle and humble in heart, and you will find rest for your souls. For my yoke is easy and my burden is light."

We take comfort in your words and draw close to find our rest in you.
Amen.

16) Prayer for parents of adult children:

I am in great need of your guidance, Lord.
Being a parent of adult children is so much harder than I thought it would be.
I thought it would be the easiest stage of all and it is definitely not.
I find like Paul that I am doing the things I ought not to do and saying the things I ought not to say. And I am doing this over and over again.
Help me keep my mouth closed and have control over my facial expressions.
Help me to withhold my opinions and my "guidance" until I am asked for help.
In this murky and slippery stage, help me to find firmer ground.

17) Prayer for parents of little ones during extremely difficult times:

I pray for all the parents of little ones. I pray that they will be able to overcome and to compensate for what they have lost during these past months of learning to live with this world-wide contagion.
I pray for those who are caring for the physical needs of our little ones…for patience and supernatural love and an abundance of wisdom.
Restore the balance in these children's lives and the lives of all who love them.

18) Prayer for the homeless:

Open our hearts, Lord.
Open our minds to understand the needs of those who have no homes, no food, no clothing or shelter…and those who have no homeland.
Help us to see their many needs and to know how we can make a difference.
Give us the means to help and give us the generosity to follow through.
Amen.

19) Prayer for the need to surrender:

Lord, we need to surrender to your will. And yet we are your reluctant children, born with stubbornness in our souls.
We know that You want us to depend fully on You. But we want to use the talents you gave us to be independent and act as if we did it all by ourselves.
Thank you for never giving up on us, for reminding us of your love and patience.
Help us to know that our strength and self-reliance come from you.
Help us to balance the pull of our egos with the strength that comes from surrender.
Thank you for being our Holy, Almighty God!

20) Prayer of thankfulness:

Lord, I thank you:
-For all the times you are there for me in the middle of the night, steadying me as I try to shake off manic thoughts and

grotesque nightmares.
-For all the times you reassure me as I drive in dangerous traffic.
-For all the times you remind me of your promises and let me know I am not alone.
-For all the times you point me back to the second chances.
-For all the times I speak or behave in ways that make you sad and you still show mercy.
-For all the times I neglect to thank you and you still continue to offer your gifts.
-For when you wash my sins away and look at them no more.
For all those times, I thank you, Lord.

21) Prayer of gratitude:

Lord, when I see the skies darken and the leaves turn in anticipation of a coming storm, let me know that you are in control of all the storms in my life.
Thank you for a peek into heaven every time I look at the night sky.
When I look closely at the blooms on the daisies in my yard and notice the spiky centers with their hundred shades of brown, let me remember that you know every cell in my body, every hair on my head.
When I draw pleasure from the soft moss in the ravines, let me know who placed it there in my path. Let me be assured of Your presence everywhere I wander.
For all these things and so much more, let me be grateful.
Amen.

22) A Simple Prayer for the New Year

We pray for renewal of energy and purpose in this new year.
We ask that all our steps be placed exactly in the path you have for us.
We pray for kindness and truth to prevail in everything we say and do.
We pray to make a difference in the lives of others and be a safe haven for all who need us.

Amen.

23) Prayer for Peace:

Lord, you are our Prince of Peace!
We ask for peace in our world, our country, and in our neighborhoods.
In our families and in our friendships.
We pray for peace in our hearts, for that is where it must begin.
Thank you for those moments when peace comes close and settles in.
Amen.

24) Prayers for when we go out into the world.

As we go out into the world, I pray that we will have eyes to see the miracles around us; ears to hear the voices of those who need us most, and the courage to do whatever it takes to transform this world into a better one.
I pray that we will work toward a more loving world, where those who have plenty will give to those who need the most; where all will feel welcome and respected, no matter their beliefs, their age, gender, race or culture.

I pray that we will look up and all around to see His wonders in the sky both day and night, and that we can take those wonders into our lives and feel refreshed and whole again.
I pray that we will be renewed and connected by the things that matter most.
Amen.

The End

Three months ago, I started dabbling with watercolors. Scrolling through Instagram, I saw a video of someone painting flowers. Classical music was playing in the background and I was hooked by the flow of the brush and the skilled blending of colors.

I foraged through my basement and found a box marked "Kid's Crafts". Eight years ago, when I downsized my home, I gave away designer lamps and antique vases, but kept this box. You can call me crazy. I wouldn't blame you. But I did a little victory dance when I retrieved a container of crumbly watercolors, some scraggly brushes, and a plastic palette.

I hurried upstairs to fill a bowl with water and ventured to bring the paints and a neglected part of myself back to life.

Have I discovered the hidden Monet in me? No. But the elation I feel when I dip my brush into the pool of pigments, and mix 4 different colors to create that particular shade of silver-blue found on spruce trees, might rival what my pickle-ball friends feel when they smash one over the net.

I've been painting hydrangeas, sunflowers, daisies, roses, trees, sunsets, and lots of leaves. I'm in love with everything about it. It's simultaneously relaxing and stimulating. Each time the tip of my paint-loaded brush, touches the water on the canvas, the explosion of color and movement is magical. And every now and then, what is left on my canvas is worth saving.

Good things happen when we discover new passions or recover old dreams.

Which box we save, what colors we choose, which people we cherish, what paths we take, all lead to the marks we make with the time we have.

What is left on our canvasses is what matters most.

About the Author

I started my career writing and teaching, and I ended it much the same. I taught high school literature, directed plays and musicals, managed multiple departments in banking and insurance, and finally led a Human Resources department. I loved each position. All of them contributed to the rewarding role of 'late in life' motherhood. In my 20's, I acted in community theater, with parts in *Godspell*, *Any Wednesday*, *Gaslight,* and *Adam and Eve,* Mark Twain's satire. I love walking in any weather, especially with my grand dog, Pepper, painting with watercolors, making wreaths, preparing good food for people I love, sipping wine or cocoa around a firepit, visiting family and spending time with friends. While I come from a family of Welsh brooders and can plum the depths of any emotion, I end up on the side of enthusiastic optimists. No matter the season you'll find me outside following the moon and looking up at the stars.

WA

Made in the USA
Monee, IL
01 July 2023